NASCAR

A Week in the Life of NASCAR
A View from Within

Unrestricted Access to the Lives of Teams, Crews and Drivers

TRIUMPH
B O O K S
CHICAGO

Printed in U.S.A.
ISBN-13: 978-1-57243-794-4
ISBN-10: 1-57243-794-4

Library of Congress Control Number:
2005906354

Designed by Valerie Deri Helvey

Cover helmet courtesy of
Team Simpson Racing.
Helmet design and artwork by
R. Powell (airbrushguy.com).
Photo by Jim Fluharty.

This book is available in quantity at
special discounts for your group or
organization. For further information,
contact:

Triumph Books
542 South Dearborn Street
Suite 750
Chicago, Illinois 60605
(312) 939-3330
Fax (312) 663-3557

ACCESS GRANTED

Approaching the creation of this book, we wanted to offer NASCAR fans a peek behind the curtain to experience the inner workings of America's fastest growing and most popular spectator sport. Somewhere along the line, though, we tore the curtain from its rod, burned it and kicked down the door to a world that has long been locked from public view.

Fully aware of the "this-has-never-been-done-before" resistance we might face, my assistants, Jay Pfeifer and Will Conroy, and I embarked on a quest to produce the most comprehensive behind-the-scenes examination of NASCAR ever attempted.

Welcome to *A Week in the Life of NASCAR: A View from Within*.

As you peruse these pages, you are taken places and witness elements of racing that, until now, have been hidden behind Do Not Enter and Authorized Personnel Only signs.

We decided to bookend this experience with the NASCAR NEXTEL Cup races at Talladega and Darlington, two of NASCAR's most notorious and vastly different tracks. At the tracks, you are invited to check out prerace inspections, practice and qualifying. You walk the garage as adjustments are made, spend time in team and drivers meetings and have an insider's view of the pageantry of prerace festivities.

Once the green flag drops, life in the pits and post-wreck repairs are yours to savor.

After both races, we take you to victory lane and through postrace inspections – including the complete breakdown of Jeff Gordon's victorious No. 24 at Talladega – something never before seen. From there, we pack up and travel home with our teams.

In the days leading up to and between the races, we take you to three shops for an insider's look at what it takes to prepare cars, teams and drivers for the challenges of stock car racing at its highest level. You visit the wind tunnel – usually off-limits to media and fans – to see what happens and how cars are adjusted based on the data generated. We take you to a day of testing at Lowe's Motor Speedway and to pit practices where crews work to shave milliseconds from their stops.

Although the NASCAR NEXTEL Cup Series calendar is defined by a 10-month, 36-race schedule, stock car racing is actually a year-round, 24/7 grind. For the people who live it every day, there is much more to NASCAR than what is shown during weekend telecasts.

It is our hope that this book not only entertains in words and images, but also exposes fans to what it really takes to compete in NASCAR's premier series.

As in any competitive industry, changes in personnel are common. Because this book is a 12-day time capsule, no editorial adjustments were made to account for changes in sponsorships or personnel that occurred in the weeks and months following the conclusion of our adventure.

I must offer a special thanks to the fine folks at NASCAR, Hendrick Motorsports, MB2/MBV Motorsports and Haas CNC Racing. Without their support and enthusiasm, this project would not have been possible.

We hope you enjoy this behind-the-scenes experience as much as we enjoyed living it.

Tighten those belts,

Michael J. Fresina

Michael J. Fresina
Publisher – Executive Editor
Street & Smith's Specialty Publications

A Week in the Life of NASCAR
A View from Within

Unrestricted Access to the Lives of Teams, Crews and Drivers

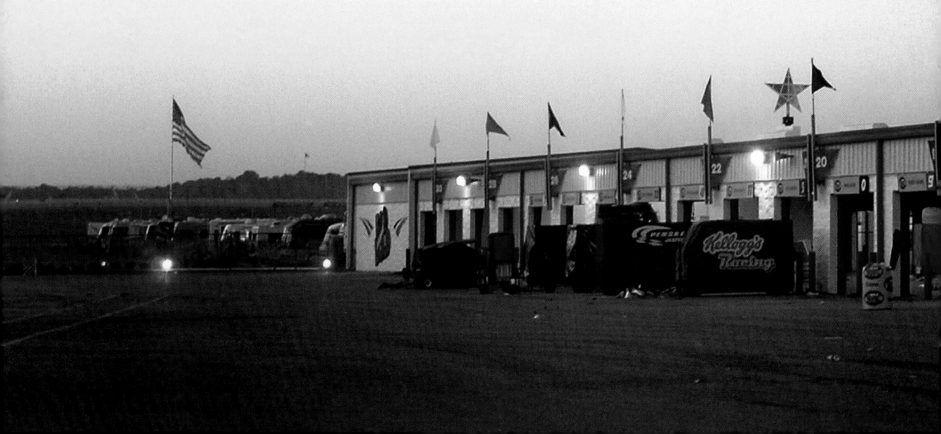

FOREWORD

Brian France................ 8

TALLADEGA

**Legendary Track Delivers
Another Classic** 11

PRERACE

• Anxious Hours 12

RACE

• The Big One................. 23

POSTRACE

• Final Exam.................. 30

THE LIFE

A Peek Behind the Curtain...41

THE SHOP

• Where It All Begins 43

PIT PRACTICE

• Beat The Clock 50

WIND TUNNEL

• Ride The Wind 55

TESTING

• Pushing Limits 58

DOWNTIME

• Lovin' Every Minute Of It 63

PUBLIC PROPERTY

• Everyone Gets A Piece 66

Q&A

**Chatting With the People
Who Make NASCAR Go**..... 77

• Hendrick Motorsports.......... 78

• MB2/MBV Motorsports 103

• Haas CNC Racing............ 126

DARLINGTON

Still Too Tough To Tame.... 139

PRERACE

• Early Action 140

RACE

• Into The Night 151

POSTRACE

• Mama, I'm Coming Home 158

NASCAR
Inside the Experience

Anyone who has watched a NASCAR race, either live or on television, can attest to the on-track excitement of our sport, which is obvious. Something that's not as obvious, though, is the action behind the scenes, involving all the members of all the teams who work long, hard hours to give their respective drivers a chance to roll into victory lane.

A Week in the Life of NASCAR offers readers *A View from Within* to learn what it takes to succeed at stock car racing's highest level. Street & Smith's Specialty Publications and NASCAR – in conjunction with Triumph Books – have combined to bring you this one-of-a-kind publication.

You don't just read *A Week in the Life of NASCAR*. You *experience* it.

After all, you don't just watch NASCAR. You *experience* it.

The focus of these pages is a week-long stretch of activity encompassing two of NASCAR's legendary race tracks – Talladega Superspeedway and Darlington Raceway. As you'll find, these races were a great choice for this book, because while Talladega and Darlington both have a rich history and long-standing popularity, they have little in common when it comes to the actual competition they produce. Each is unique, and the fact that their spring races are held back-to-back creates a compelling challenge for our competitors in the NASCAR NEXTEL Cup Series.

That challenge comes alive in this book, where you get a close-up look at how three very different organizations – Hendrick Motorsports, MB2/MBV Motorsports and Haas CNC Racing – cope with the rigors of competition.

You see what goes on at the race shops, and how both cars and pit crew members are whipped into shape. You get a glimpse at what it takes to transport a full-scale NASCAR team from track to track.

You are given a garage pass, and this book takes you through the prerace and postrace activities, including the drivers meetings with officials and our intricate inspection process. And of course, race and pit-road action almost leaps from the page.

NASCAR got involved with this project to give our fans access to a variety of rarely seen moments. The aim was to help create something truly special.

We think that has been accomplished. I'm sure you'll feel the same way.

Best regards,

Brian France
Chairman and CEO, NASCAR

"Talladega is one of those places that will make you religious pretty quick."

Ryan Pemberton
Crew Chief – No. 01
Army Chevrolet

TALLADEGA TWIST

Legendary Track Delivers Another Classic

Everything is bigger at Talladega. Not only is it the longest NASCAR track at 2.66 miles, but with four lanes, it is one of the widest. The 33-degree corner banking and long stretches breed the fastest NASCAR NEXTEL Cup Series action, so fast that in 1988 NASCAR introduced restrictor plates to control speeds. The sprawling complex also draws a huge crowd with more than 300,000 fans making their way to the Alabama landmark. Talladega Superspeedway is truly a titan in the NASCAR world.

We will take you into the heart of the fastest race on NASCAR's biggest stage. We were there from the installation of restrictor plates to the final postrace inspection of Jeff Gordon's unbeatable car. You'll get an immersive view of race weekend and go where even a Hot Pass can't take you. Look into a team's hauler for the prerace pep talk and visit the garage after The Big One. And stand by as our teams try to bounce back from one of the largest wrecks in NASCAR history. ▲

Fast and furious: Racing at The 'Dega is often a blur.

ANXIOUS HOURS
Stress Defines Talladega Prerace

ABOVE: NASCAR officials use templates to ensure Joe Nemechek's Chevrolet conforms to the proper specifications.

OPPOSITE: No Speeding: Restrictor plates – required by NASCAR – limit a car's speed by controlling the airflow from the carburetor to the engine.

At the granddaddy of all superspeedways, a strong car is the key to victory. Even the drivers will tell you that no wheelman can make up for a slow car at The 'Dega. With so much pressure to produce a fast car at Talladega, NASCAR has to be vigilant to prevent cheaters from gaining an unfair advantage.

We'll take you through the entire prerace ritual. You'll watch as teams are given engine-choking restrictor plates and crew chiefs select shocks and springs. You'll see NASCAR officials take each of our team's cars through template checks to make sure every inch of the car meets NASCAR's specs.

Once the cars check out, you'll watch the drivers and the teams get ready for the big race. What do teams say before the race? What do drivers eat before getting behind the wheel? The answers are within. ▲

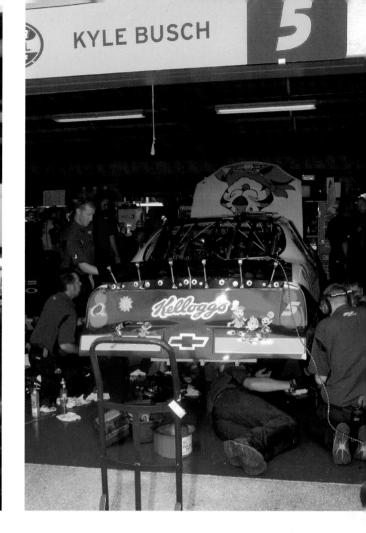

KYLE BUSCH 5

LEFT and TOP: Garage time: Teams make final adjustments to cars before qualifying.

ABOVE: An Army of Many: With a little help from Martha Nemechek, Joe's mom, the No. 01 team guides their car to the garage for inspection.

ABOVE: Hangin' around: Crew chief Ryan Pemberton passes the time while the No. 01 car is put through the rigorous inspection process.

RIGHT: So many to choose from: The Army team selects their springs and gets ready for installation.

OPPOSITE: Don't even think about it: NASCAR president Mike Helton keeps a watchful eye for cheaters as the cars pass through inspection.

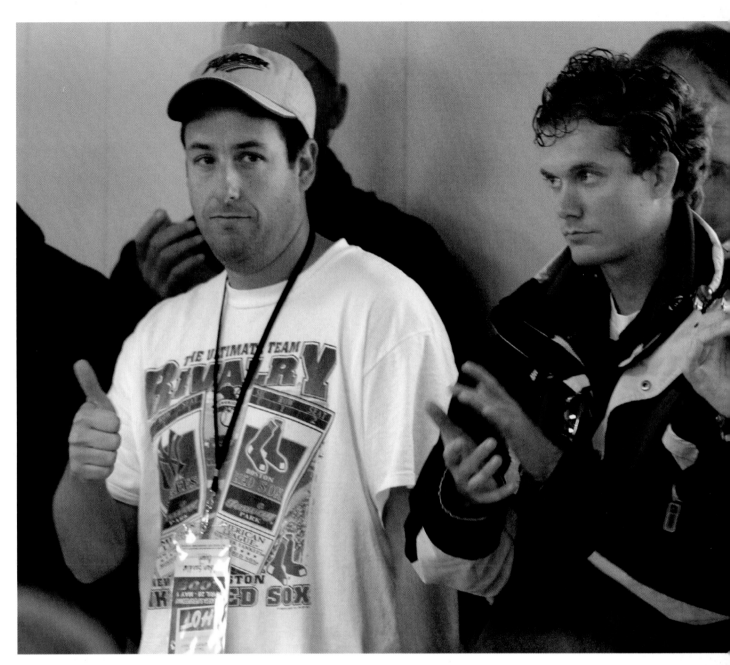

LEFT: Listen up: Drivers and crew chiefs receive their final instructions before the race begins.

ABOVE: Adam Sandler, honorary grand marshal, keeps the jokes to a minimum during the drivers meeting.

ABOVE: Scott Riggs shovels in his prerace staple – chicken and pasta.

OPPOSITE: "Alright, boys. *FOCUS* on three!" Crew chief Doug Randolph
has the No. 10 team ready to roll.

THE BIG ONE
Record Crash Overshadows Gordon Win

Even the crashes are bigger at Talladega. With cars traveling in a single pack, just inches apart at breakneck speed, one twitch – a momentary lapse in concentration – can result in The Big One. That's exactly what happened in the 2005 Aaron's 499.

The Big One started out small – as little more than a puff of smoke entering Turn 1 – but quickly escalated. After a few seconds of screeching tires, scraping metal and uneasy breathing, Talladega had dashed the hopes of 25 teams on lap 132, including Scott Riggs, who was in sixth place when the accident occurred.

After the wreck, the garage became a blur of activity as teams struggled to get their cars back on the track. Once the race resumed, with many teams still pounding dents and replacing parts, teammates Jeff Gordon and Jimmie Johnson battled for the lead.

After a late caution, the action-packed day climaxed with a green-white-checkered finish. Jeff Gordon, who led for 139 of the 194 laps, held off the hard-charging Tony Stewart to capture his second consecutive victory at the Alabama superspeedway. ▲

OPPOSITE: The Big One.

ABOVE: Leader of the pack: Jeff Gordon holds the lead as others work the draft.

OPPOSITE: With action on the track, the garage and haulers yawn with emptiness.

LEFT: Little more...little more...right there! Over-the-wall pit crews stretch out before the first pit stop.

BELOW: Immediately after a pit stop, Kellogg's crew members carefully record the wear on each tire and then report to the crew chief.

BOTTOM: Scott Riggs runs in front of Jimmie Johnson and Tony Stewart.

CLOCKWISE FROM TOP LEFT:

All banged up: The Army team works furiously to get the No. 01 back into racing shape.

Rookie Kyle Busch addresses the media after a disappointing DNF.

It's okay, Dad: Little John Hunter consoles his father as the team tries to repair the Army car.

With the media watching, Scott Riggs' crew assesses the damage to the No. 10 car before beginning repairs.

Is that crayon? Scott Riggs returns to the track with a new quarter panel – and a faux number – after his car got banged around during The Big One.

No. 10 car chief Rodney Childers seeks emergency care after slicing his hand during repairs.

Teamwork: Eight members of the Valvoline crew work on one side of the mangled car.

Who knows a welder? After slamming into the wall, Scott Riggs' No. 10 Valvoline is barely recognizable.

Game over: The No. 5 car is towed back to the Kellogg's hauler after getting caught in The Big One.

ABOVE: Here they come: All eyes follow the action as the pack moves out of Turn 4 and onto the frontstretch.

RIGHT & OPPOSITE: Dominating The 'Dega: After holding off a late charge from Tony Stewart and Michael Waltrip, Jeff Gordon claims his second consecutive victory at Talladega.

FINAL EXAM
Teams Take Off, Gordon Inspected

ABOVE: This way please: Jeff Gordon steers his No. 24 Chevrolet into victory lane.

OPPOSITE: Champion! Jeff Gordon and crew celebrate their victory in the Aaron's 499.

As the stands emptied and the sun dipped below the horizon, teams hurried to begin the second-most important race of the day – a sprint to their waiting airplanes. Within minutes of the checkered flag, they closed the pits, emptied the garages and loaded the haulers.

While the teams flew home, truck drivers were just getting started. Staring down a long drive, they would arrive at team headquarters eight hours later, ending a very long weekend.

One team, however, did not have the luxury of an early departure. After a trip to victory lane and through a gauntlet of sponsor photos, the No. 24 team stayed behind to shepherd their car through a final battery of technical checks.

NASCAR officials templated and measured the car, then disassembled the engine and suspension. If the winning car were illegal in any way, NASCAR would have found it. After clearing inspection, Gordon and his team headed home to get ready for Darlington.

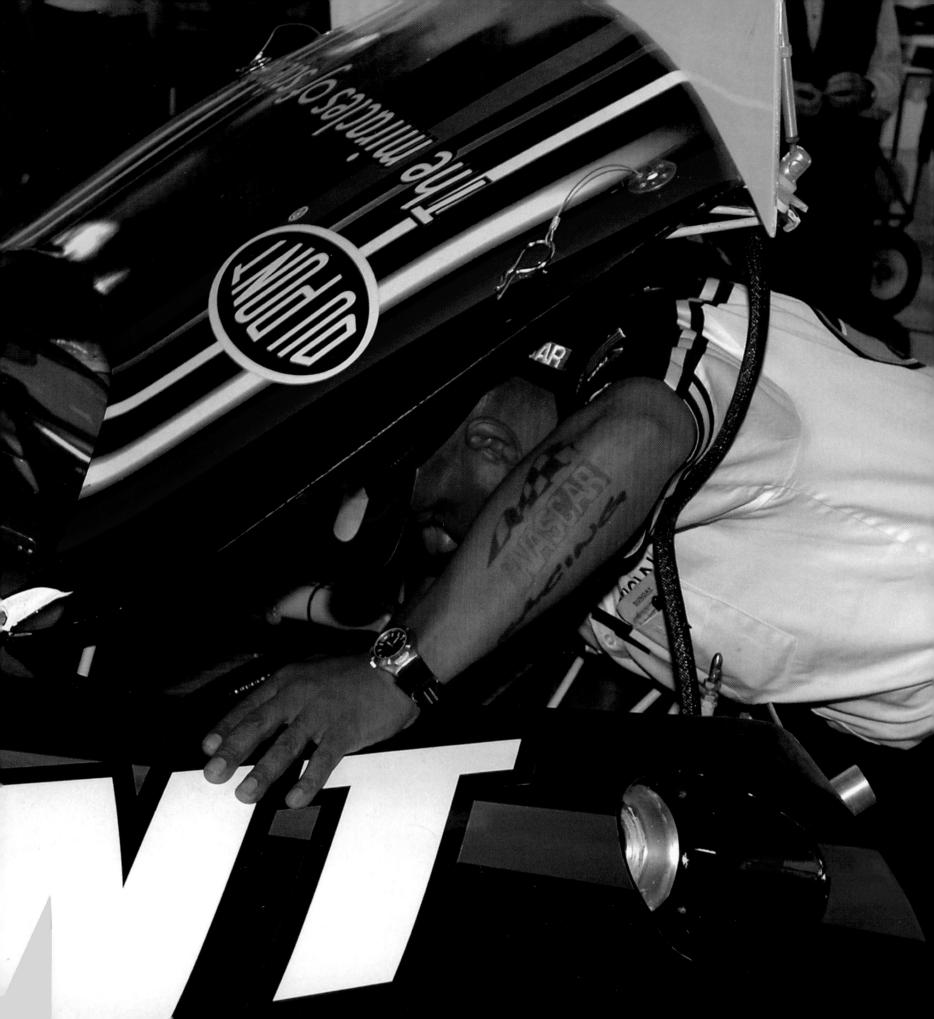

OPPOSITE: True fan: Dean Duckett, a technical inspector, *really* likes NASCAR.

LEFT: You have to be at least THIS TALL to pass inspection.

BELOW: Flanked by officials the No. 24 makes its way from one inspection to the next.

BOTTOM: Measuring up: NASCAR officials lay the body templates on the No. 24 car to ensure it meets all required standards.

ABOVE: Jeff Gordon, the victor, on his way to check out postrace inspection.

RIGHT: Jeff Gordon's winning car sits on jack stands as the undercarriage is examined.

FAR LEFT TOP AND BOTTOM: That's a wrap: After a disappointing finish, the No. 10 team packs and closes the hauler before heading back to Concord, NC.

LEFT: All over but the sweepin'.

TOP: It's good to be last: With the stands and garages empty, but with the winner's trophy in hand, the DuPont Chevrolet is the last car packed away.

ABOVE: "1, 2, 3, RANDY": The victorious No. 24 team pauses to remember Randy Dorton before heading back to North Carolina.

OPPOSITE: Safe at home: The No. 24 hauler is a blur as it arrives back at Hendrick Motorsports.

LEFT: Back at Hendrick Motorsports, truck driver Dave Radney begins unloading the No. 25 hauler in the pre-dawn hours.

BOTTOM: Keep out.

EMPLOYEES
ONLY
NO DELIVERIES
AT THIS GATE

PRIVATE
PROPERTY
NO TRESPASSING

"...the current grind really beats up the guys who live this life."

Doug Randolph
Crew Chief – No. 10
Valvoline Chevrolet

THE LIFE
A Peek Behind the Curtain

R acing is much more than speed, pit stops and trophies. At its highest level, stock car racing is a multi-billion-dollar international business – and, as in any industry, success is dictated by activities performed far from the limelight.

The calendars of every NASCAR team are measured in hours at the shop – days and nights spent searching for new ideas to put the team back in victory lane. With the competition always on your rear bumper, life in NASCAR is a 'round-the-clock, year-in, year-out battle.

In this section, we take you into the shops for a first-hand look at the struggle for survival in the NASCAR jungle. You're invited to stroll through the garage, take in pit practice, visit the wind tunnel and go to testing.

You'll also tag along with NASCAR's rock stars as they hang out, meet their fans, deal with the media and court sponsors.

To conclude this look at The Life of NASCAR, we offer the thoughts of 30 people who live it everyday. ▲

Feeding frenzy: NASCAR's pulse is always racing.

WHERE IT ALL BEGINS
The Shop: Racing's Nerve Center

Hanging bodies, mounting engines, loading haulers – and everything else that goes into building a race car – takes place at the shop.

Constructing high-tech machines that roar around race tracks each week is as expensive as it is complex. At any given time, each team is developing 14-17 cars (costing upwards of $100,000 each), with the guys implementing strategies and setups for races that are weeks away.

Shops themselves have become mini-factories and vary greatly in size and complexity.

Hendrick Motorsports sits on a sprawling campus, which includes twin 86,000-square-foot NASCAR NEXTEL Cup shops as well as administrative buildings, a museum and expansive retail store. By comparison, single-car teams like Haas CNC Racing operate in more modest facilities.

Teams employ at least 40 shop workers, each responsible for a specific aspect of the car. Job descriptions vary, but each person shares a common goal: To produce a car bound for victory lane. ▲

OPPOSITE: Skeleton Crew: Even the car's bones get touch-up paint.

ABOVE: The Army team working on four of their 17 race cars.

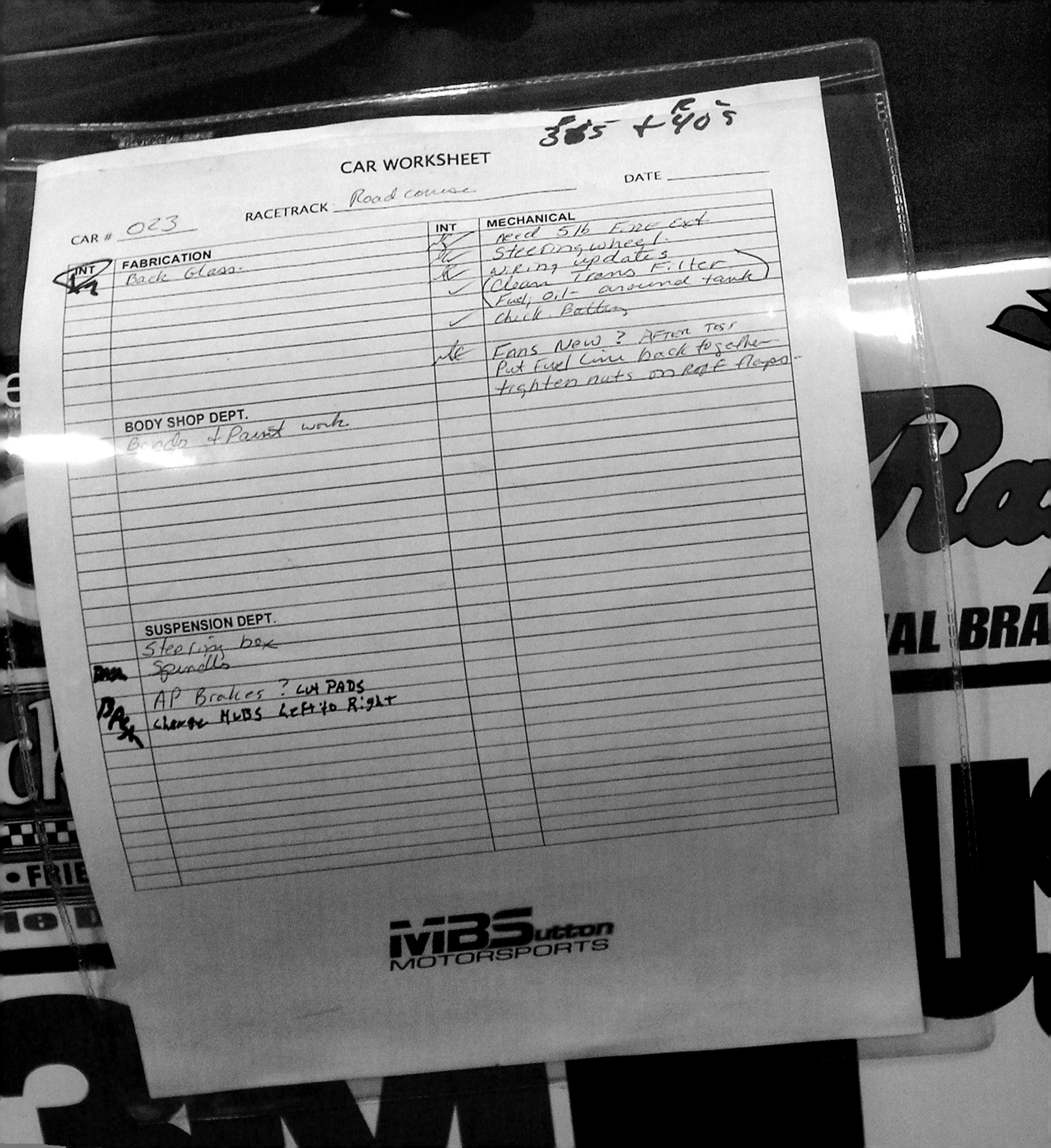

385 + 40s (handwritten top)

CAR WORKSHEET

RACETRACK _Road course_   DATE _____

CAR # _023_

INT	MECHANICAL
✓	need 5/6 Fire Ext
✓	Steering wheel.
✓	wiring updates
	(Clean Trans Filter
	Fuel, oil - around tank)
✓	check Battery
te	Fans New ? After Test
	Put Fuel line back together
	tighten nuts on Roof flaps -

(INT) FABRICATION
Back Glass.

BODY SHOP DEPT.
Binder + Paint work

SUSPENSION DEPT.
Steering box
Spindles
AP Brakes ? low PADS
check MUBS Left to Right

MBSutton MOTORSPORTS

OPPOSITE: Road course worksheet:
The ultimate to-do list.

ABOVE: Power play: The quest for 200 mph
starts right here.

BOTTOM LEFT: A work in progress.

BELOW: Kevin Sigafoos, front-tire carrier,
also works as a mechanic on the No. 25.

45

CLOCKWISE FROM TOP LEFT:

Engineer Brian Zeck pores over data to optimize the No. 10 car's performance.

Shane Cooke adjusts each of Scott Riggs' custom-fit seats before they are installed.

Underwriter: No. 01 car chief Mark Bieberich makes final notes on the undercarriage.

Doug Morgan files the leg braces for Scott Riggs' seat.

SHHHHH: Adam Wright applies some super-secret Go-Fast Sauce.

OPPOSITE: Uh, I think you missed a spot: Jim Pollard and Mike Knauer polish the hauler.

TOP LEFT: Casey Hill and George Nelson stripe Johnson's ride.

TOP RIGHT: Three more...Two more: NASCAR Busch Series driver Boston Reid feels the burn in the Hendrick gym.

BELOW: 2 for 1: The No. 24 and No. 48 – two of NASCAR's best – reside under the same roof on the Hendrick Motorsports campus.

BEAT THE CLOCK
Pit Practice, A Test of Time

ABOVE: Hendrick Motorsports pit coach Mark Mauldin checks the clock.

OPPOSITE: Don't bother looking both ways – just cross!

Live pit stops are orchestrated chaos, micro-ballets danced in a cyclone of flammable liquids, power tools and adrenaline. The sub-15-second pit stop, once the equivalent of the four-minute mile, is no longer good enough. Today, seven grown men, eight unwieldy tires, two air wrenches, a jack and a pair of gas cans move in calculated harmony and regularly execute four-tire, full-gas and adjustment stops in under 13 seconds. Without constant practice and relentless refinement, such precision would be impossible.

Success is measured in tenth- and hundredth-of-a-second improvements. Crews are praised and prodded as their techniques are tweaked and tuned. ▲

OPPOSITE TOP: Out with the old, in with the new.

OPPOSITE BOTTOM: Wait for it: No. 01 Jackman Scott King readies for a practice run.

LEFT: Sweating the details.

ABOVE: No. 5 Jackman Rick Pigeon takes flight.

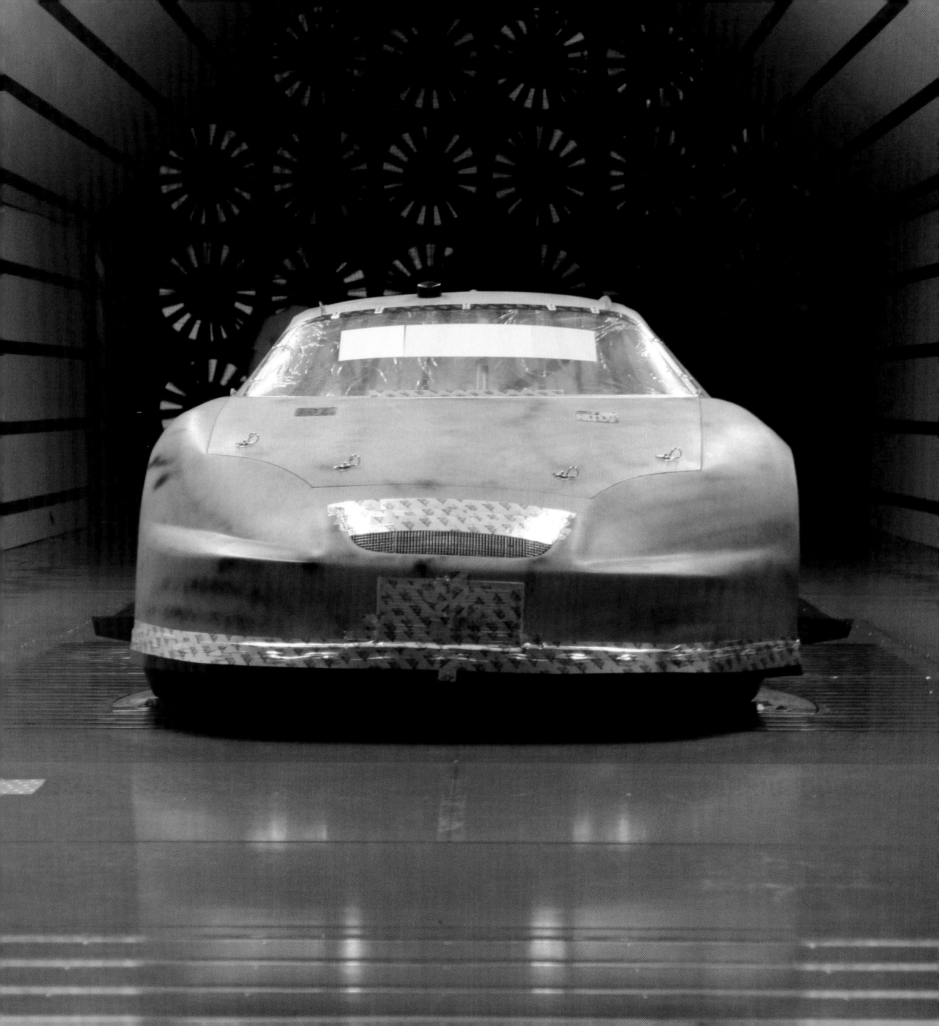

RIDE THE WIND
Tunnel Testing at AeroDyn

Although an hour can cost more than $1,200.00, NASCAR teams take their cars to the wind tunnel as often as time and resources allow. Trips to Mooresville, NC-based AeroDyn are precious to teams looking for an edge.

A full-scale closed-jet testing facility specifically designed for stock cars, AeroDyn's tunnel is more than 50 feet long, 11 feet tall and 19 feet wide. AeroDyn recreates track conditions with rollers in the floor to mimic tire movement and 22 individually speed-controlled fans that can draw wind over a test vehicle at more than 125 mph. A host

of sensors provide race teams with the most accurate information regarding downforce, front and rear drag and many more aerodynamic characteristics. The information then helps the team determine how a particular car will behave in every imaginable race scenario.

AeroDyn does not evaluate results or make suggestions. The staff provides each team with the expertise to make the most of its time at the facility, but what teams choose to do with it is of little concern to AeroDyn.

On this day, the Haas CNC Racing crew brought one of its No. 0 NetZero Best Buy Chevrolets to AeroDyn and put it through its paces. ▲

OPPOSITE: Fully loaded.

ABOVE: With wheels spinning, the car is prepared for the first test.

Getting up to speed.

CLOCKWISE FROM TOP LEFT:

AeroDyn's Ron Tucker records the car's exact location within the tunnel to ensure that future tests can be conducted and compared with great precision.

Between tests, measurements are taken and adjustments made.

Command Central: The guys from Haas CNC Racing check out the data as it is generated.

Heading home. Winded.

PUSHING LIMITS
Testing at Lowe's Motor Speedway

ABOVE: Jeff Gordon makes his final run of the day.

OPPOSITE: Fast or *flame* fast? Gordon must choose.

Over the course of two beautiful spring days, many of NASCAR's finest teams descended upon Lowe's Motor Speedway for open testing. Drivers pushed their limits on one of the circuit's fastest tracks and got their footing on the freshly levigated surface. But most important, teams were trying to find the right car and the best set-up for the NASCAR NEXTEL All-Star Challenge and the Coca-Cola 600, both just weeks away.

Usually, teams test in relative isolation on cold tracks. However, enough cars were roaring through the corners in Charlotte that

a healthy – and race-condition-replicating – layer of rubber was laid down.

The action was fast and furious with as many as ten teams vying for time, taking laps and turning heads. Each team took advantage of the close quarters, keeping an eye on the competition.

Five of our teams visited the track: Jeff Gordon's No. 24, Kyle Busch's No. 5, Brian Vickers' No. 25, Joe Nemechek's No. 01 and Mike Bliss' No. 0.

Scott Riggs' No. 10 team returned home early from Richmond, VA after their second day of testing was rained out. ▲

OPPOSITE: Jeff Gordon imparts some wisdom to teammate and NASCAR NEXTEL Cup rookie, Kyle Busch.

ABOVE: The No. 10 team returns home after a second day of testing in Richmond was rained out.

RIGHT: Mike Bliss takes to the track.

DOWNTIME
Lovin' Every Minute of It

When Loverboy cranked out the '80s blue-collar anthem *Working for the Weekend*, the headband-clad Canadians certainly didn't have NASCAR's drivers and crew chiefs in mind. In fact, had the band been thinking of the folks who make stock car racing rock, they might have been trapped by a tongue-twister of a title: *Working for Two Hours on Tuesday Evening and Wednesdays Before it's Time to Travel.*

While most people are just stretching their legs on weekend mornings, these guys are already at work, preparing to put lives and careers on the line for the entertainment of

millions. When families pack minivans for weekends of soccer games, NASCAR's finest pack themselves into firesuits and go to work.

For drivers and crew chiefs, time away from the shop and car is precious. Stringing free seconds and minutes into hours of family time is a science mastered by only the most organized of NASCAR's weekend warriors.

At the track, motorcoaches and lounges in team haulers provide relief from the stress of racing, but the best sanctuary is home, where time can be spent doing whatever one wants – or nothing at all. ▲

OPPOSITE: Doug Randolph pitches to his daughter Morgan and prays this doesn't become an *America's Funniest Videos* moment.

ABOVE: Scott Riggs, his wife Jai and son Layne sit down in the motorcoach for a little Scrabble.

CLOCKWISE FROM TOP LEFT:

Even on the links, Brian Vickers must always be accessible, this time for a radio interview.

Crew chief Ryan Pemberton likes to spend time on the lake with his wife Andrea and daughter Payton.

A day at the beach: Vickers digs out of the bunker.

Doug Randolph takes to the lake with his daughter Morgan and son Nick.

OPPOSITE: Payton Pemberton goes for a dog smooch from the sandbox.

PUBLIC PROPERTY
Sponsors, Fans and Media:
Everyone Gets a Piece

ABOVE: Chad Knaus and the rest of today's crew chiefs are as recognizable and in-demand as the drivers.

OPPOSITE: Even a Stormtrooper can't keep the media away from Jeff Gordon.

Access has always been NASCAR's trump card – its currency for generating fans, satisfying sponsors and attracting media attention.

Race fans can peek behind the curtain more freely than in any other sport, getting up close and personal with their heroes during garage tours and appearances. Today, even crew chiefs, team owners and pit crewmen find themselves the subject of fan adoration.

Likewise, sponsors expect their significant, sustaining investments to buy more than a car with their name and pretty logos on it. They are paying for a relationship with the driver, team and sport.

As stock car racing has grown out of its regional following, media coverage has exploded. Today, NASCAR issues hundreds of media credentials promising access.

This kind of access comes with a high price tag: Privacy is now a luxury the drivers cannot afford. Join us for a tour of the gauntlet of sponsors, fans and media that NASCAR's most notable figures must navigate. ▲

OPPOSITE: Joe's mom, Martha, is very involved in the Army sponsorship and has become a fan-favorite at every track.

ABOVE: Just hours before the Talladega race, Kyle Busch visits with sponsors. On this day, Busch celebrated his 20th birthday with the people from CarQuest.

LEFT: Terry Labonte shoots a commercial for Pizza Hut.

BELOW: Souvenir Alley: Sponsors love the exposure NASCAR offers.

OPPOSITE: Sign and move...sign and move.

ABOVE: Fan-tasy camp: Scott Riggs takes on fans and Valvoline reps in a kart.

LEFT: Writer's cramp: Brian Vickers autographs cards for fans.

ABOVE: Mike Bliss meets with fans at a local Best Buy.

RIGHT: Kyle Busch poses with a young fan at his souvenir trailer.

OPPOSITE: Sometimes, I swear, it seems like people are staring at me.

OPPOSITE: Youth movement: It's not every day that a member of the media makes 20-year-old Kyle Busch feel old. Here, 12-year-old Joe'l Jeter interviews Busch for SC-ETV's *Deputy Billy and Friends*.

ABOVE: Before qualifying, Joe Nemechek takes a minute to talk with TV reporters.

LEFT: Brian Vickers takes the media spotlight head-on.

"What we do back here at the shop, and the size of the circus that we run, is unknown to a lot of fans."

Ryan Pemberton
Crew Chief – No. 01
Army Chevrolet

One on One: Brian Vickers fields questions from publisher, Michael Fresina.

E ven though TV may not show them, radio doesn't interview them and newspapers don't write much about them, NASCAR teams employ hundreds of behind-the-scenes people. These racers perform jobs big and small, each with eyes set on victory lane. While drivers and crew chiefs enjoy their ever-expanding celebrity, there are hundreds of people, critical to NASCAR's success, who live and work just outside of the limelight.

We took our tape recorders and cameras beyond the press conferences and personal appearances – beyond what is obvious – and into the heart of racing.

We conducted Q&A's with people from every level of the NASCAR food chain. From drivers and crew chiefs to the shop workers and "carpetwalkers" (folks who rarely make it to the track but play an essential role in making it all possible); they're all here. This is a true 360-degree view of racing; these are the people who fuel NASCAR.

Having the opportunity to sit down, one-on-one, with some of racing's most- and least-recognizable figures, we came away with a much deeper understanding of NASCAR and so will you. ▲

Jimmie Johnson

Driver – No. 48
Lowe's Chevrolet

How is Talladega unique?

At Talladega and Daytona, you spend 90 percent of your time playing defense and 10 percent playing offense. It's just how the draft works.

Usually, you look forward and pay attention, thinking about how to drive by the guy in front of you. You can't do that at Talladega. You need to have help from behind, so it is the complete opposite of what we are used to. It's defensive.

Restrictor-plate racing is all about not getting passed, not letting somebody get position on you. You have to block, look in the mirror and keep people behind you.

With your schedule, how are you handling being a newlywed?

In some ways, I think my schedule lets us spend more time together. Granted, we aren't at home and sometimes we wish we had a normal routine, but we don't. We are always on the road, traveling, doing new and exciting things.

In the grand scheme of things, we actually spend quite a bit of time together. Granted, a lot of it is in airplanes, or riding in the motorcoach.

There are times during the season when we will just cancel what is going on and say, "We are going home. We miss it. We need to be home."

How involved were you in your wedding plans or decorating the house?

I know what I *don't* like and am not afraid to be opinionated. I was involved with the wedding to a certain degree. There was stuff I wasn't in favor of.

When it comes to decorating and picking materials, there is a lot of give and take. The place needs to be *ours*. I am not creative, but my wife is awesome with that. She has incredible style, so she is able to really pull it

together and I'm more the guy who comes along and says, "Well, I'm not really sure about that…"

I think at times I frustrate her because I spend more time telling her what I don't like than clueing her in on things I do like.

What is your dream day off?

I would be down on an island, in the sand and water, just sitting in the sun relaxing. Just chilling, doing nothing. We do too much, so doing nothing is fun.

We got married on the island of St. Bart's, so that is one of our favorite places.

What do you eat before races?

I think people train their stomachs to handle different things, but for myself, I really just do a lot of pasta loading. I try to keep the energy up. What I've been doing lately is eating energy bars during the race under caution. During a pit stop, someone will pass one to me in the car. It has really boosted my energy level towards the end of a race.

If you had a CD player in the car, what would you play?

For qualifying, I need something fast and aggressive, like Metallica. The whole *Black Album* is just amazing, it never gets old.

For race day, I'd like some Jack Johnson, something with a slow, steady rhythm.

Is it true that on race day you want to operate at 80 percent intensity?

We say 80 percent, because when you try and give 100 percent, you give 120 percent, so we say 80 and land right at 100. We have to trick ourselves.

In this competition, you have to be "on" from the drop of the green flag all the way through the end, pushing the car at 100 percent.

The toughest thing is staying in control of your emotions and your intensity. It is so easy to try too hard and make mistakes.

What happens when you get angry?

Everyone has different ways of coping, depending on the circumstances. Sometimes it is easy to get over things and other times it is not. Within our team, if somebody gets out of whack, we do a good job of helping him settle back down during the race.

If I blow up, Chad [Knaus, crew chief] and the spotters try to calm me down. We try to level each other out. ▲

"... we wish we had a **normal routine,** but we don't. We are always on the road, traveling, doing new and exciting things."

"... one little thing is all it takes to ruin your Sunday."

How many engines are in development at one time?

We have a rotation of between 195 and 200 engines. Twenty-five are solely dedicated to development, which means they stay at the shop and never see a race track.

Are there a lot of trade secrets?

Yes. This is a business and you try to play things close to your vest as long as you can because you may only have two or three weeks at the track where your team has an advantage.

What do you do when an engine fails?

The first thing we do is try to understand the parameters in which the failure occurred at the track. We try to understand the conditions in which the engine ran and eliminate any factors at the track – like a hole in the radiator – that could have caused the problem.

Once we get it back to the shop, we take it apart and lay it out. Then we try to understand the sequence of events during which the failure occurred. We try to understand which component actually failed and whether or not it was a failure of that component structurally, or whether there was something else that contributed.

How different are the engines for Talladega and Darlington?

They are completely different. On the outside, they look pretty much the same, but there are quite a few differences inside. The restrictor-plate engines run at 7,500 rpm and the Darlington engine can turn 9,500 rpm, so there is quite a difference right there.

What keeps you up the night before a race?

There are all sorts of parts and pieces going around inside that engine on Sunday. Intake valves going up and down 80 times a second, and pistons going up and down 150 times a second and one little thing is all it takes to ruin your Sunday.

Jeff Andrews

**Engine Program Director
Hendrick Motorsports**

How did you get started in racing?

My family has been in racing, well, forever. Ever since I was born, my father and I have been building engines for everything from drag boats to sprint cars, all kinds of stuff. As a family, we raced on weekends.

I had an opportunity in 1988 to go to an Indy car team in Michigan and through a series of events, I ended up at Hendrick Motorsports in 1992.

Did you go to school for engineering?

I went to school, but I actually have a degree in fire science. I was going to college to be involved in the fire department and arson investigation.

I picked firefighting because it would allow me time off to go racing on weekends.

What is one thing NASCAR fans should know?

The biggest thing is that there is a lot more work than it seems from the outside. The time away from home, the travel, the hours – it is a lot of work.

And it is even more work to be competitive. You are always thinking and competing against 42 other teams that are thinking just like you. It's just non-stop. ▲

Pat Perkins

**Director of Marketing
Hendrick Motorsports**

Has Hendrick Motorsports changed a great deal since you arrived in 1999?

It has been amazing. When I first came on board, there were roughly 230 people working here – and that was a lot at the time. Now, six years later, we've got 500 employees. We've added race teams, built all these new buildings and been fortunate enough to acquire more sponsors.

As Director of Marketing, what do you do?

My job is to take care of the sponsors who support this organization. That is No. 1. That is the mission of everyone who works in a marketing capacity here, to support our partners and provide the utmost in customer service and value. That is the common thread. It is what Mr. Hendrick expects. We are in the business of fulfilling his vision.

Secondarily, I oversee the acquisition, satisfaction and retention of sponsors.

Hendrick Motorsports has two non-retail primary sponsors in GMAC and DuPont. Do you have to be more creative with them?

Actually, you have to be a lot more creative with companies that provide consumer goods and major retailers than you do with companies like GMAC and DuPont.

The interesting thing about DuPont and GMAC – really a lot of our sponsors – is that they are in it more for recognition internally than consumer sales. They are interested in building strong internal programs that they can extend to their dealers or extend to body shop owners. Those types of programs tend to be our strengths. We are very good at developing morale-based programs, employee-based programs and customer-based programs because that is the line of business that we all come from. We are most comfortable in that arena.

Are there really two sides to modern racing?

Yes, there is a competition side and there is a business side to this sport. That is how this organization is structured.

We've got a competition sector that does nothing but that. And then, we have an entire business sector, that does nothing but complement what the competition side does. And, that is really our role, we are the enabler. We are always trying to move things along and provide the competition side with the tools, resources and management so they don't have to mess with it.

We don't want the crew chiefs having to deal with this stuff. We are dealing with it. We are definitely the behind-the-scenes people that push the on-track product forward.

When it comes to merchandise with logos, do sponsors have to approve everything?

Yes. If it bears their name, they need to see it. But our drivers have some input, too. Their hats are a really big deal. Our drivers get really involved in car designs and uniforms. They have opinions, and they matter. They are wearing the hat all the time and they want something that is reflective of their style.

Do drivers need to be accessible to fans?

Yes. The France family has always been very good about that. Originally, drivers were just regular guys. Today is just an extension of the early days. The sport hasn't forgotten its roots and hasn't forgotten that the sport is still about accessibility and identification with an individual.

To me, these guys are modern-day gladiators. Racing combines the passion of the automobile, the thrill of speed, and the danger of putting those things together with a human being. There is a naturally occurring emotional connection between drivers and fans. That connection grows as a byproduct of accessibility. ▲

"To me, these guys are **modern-day gladiators.**"

Jeff Gordon

Driver – No. 24
DuPont Chevrolet

share an experience so that I can turn around and tell my friends about the conversation I had with that person – not that I just met them.

How do you balance off-track responsibilities and staying on top?

It's hard. It's hectic all the time. After Talladega, I'm spending the first couple of days doing some testing in Charlotte, and then I am going to fly up to New York City to do some PR for Tag Heuer. I'm heading straight from there to Darlington for the race weekend. It's really an around-the-clock responsibility and with the season as long as it is, it can be tough sometimes.

How has being a celebrity affected your life?

I actually don't think about it as much as I used to. At the beginning, when you see your face all over and how people act when they see you, you really don't know what to do. But over time, my perspective has changed. You just get used to feeling that way – you get comfortable.

It's funny, I'm probably more recognizable now than I ever have been, but I feel the fame a whole lot less.

What advice do you have for fans that want to approach you?

The most important thing is for them to calm down. The whole point is to take something away from the encounter. Sometimes fans get so excited that they forget what they wanted to tell me. They clearly have a specific idea or story that they want to share, but it gets lost in the excitement. It's easy to forget that when fans see me out, I'm not Jeff Gordon, the race car driver. I'm just trying to be Jeff Gordon, a normal guy.

When you meet someone you admire – and I've felt this way too when I've met celebrities on the set of *Regis and Kelly* or on *Saturday Night Live* – it's hard to keep your head. But I try to ask a question or

But when I'm not racing or doing something racing-related – which is pretty much all the time – I try to get up to New York City or down to the Bahamas to get away from it all, even for a little while.

You've raced several times at both Talladega and Darlington. Over the years, how have the races changed?

Really, not much has changed. While the cars have changed, my approach hasn't changed. You do the same things at Talladega and Darlington that you used to do a couple of years ago.

At the tracks, the only thing that has changed is the night race at Darlington but that really only changes the schedule and the car might set up and drive a bit differently if it's cooler in the evening.

What's one thing the average NASCAR fan should know - but doesn't – about racing?

[laughing] I think they know the sport better than we do most of the time. ▲

"I'm probably more recognizable now than I ever have been, **but I feel the fame a whole lot less."**

". . . the things I used to do in my 'personal time' are just not an option for me anymore. **This sport consumes you."**

What does a team manager do?

The crew chiefs and I make sure all of the logistics throughout the week are taken care of. That includes personnel issues, transportation issues, just the overall day-to-day happenings at the shop.

We also handle the actual car that goes onto the track. The engine shop gives us the engine, the chassis shop hangs the bodies, but we are the ones who finish it up and take it to the track.

How do you get the guys to work together and minimize personnel issues?

The biggest thing – like any other sport – is to look at the race as a team event. It is not that we discourage any one person from being a superstar, but each person in our building has a definite role and no one person can overshadow or dominate what is going to happen. We really emphasize communication and we make sure that everyone knows what's going on.

Communication is critical because our priorities change a great deal from day to day. On a clean sheet of paper, we know how everything is going to go, but that usually isn't how it works out.

What are some of the challenges of working on a large team?

Single-car teams are very, very straightforward. I got my start by walking in the back door of Alan Kulwicki's shop and washing the transporter. I remember people saying that working at Alan's place was good because there was just one boss – Alan.

Over here, we have crew chiefs, managers, group leaders; it is like any big corporation where there are a lot of people involved in everything. That is the biggest difference.

The people who haven't come up through racing in the straightforward model don't understand that the bottom line is that you've got to go to the race track regardless of which department fell down on the job.

What do you look for when you are hiring?

It is almost to the point that some of the decisions we make on people are based on their communication skills more so than their race car skills. They have to have both, but we put an emphasis on communication skills.

You can have a really excellent mechanic or an excellent fabricator or an excellent engineer, but if they can't communicate with the other guys on the team, that is a big handicap for them.

If there is one thing NASCAR fans need to know, what is it?

The travel and the amount of commitment required is huge. This really is much more than just a job; you don't just come to work from 9-5. It is a lifestyle and a commitment. You try to get yourself some personal time, but for me, the things I used to do in my "personal time" are just not an option for me anymore. This sport consumes you.

Brian Whitesell

Team Manager
No. 5, No. 25 and No. 44

Terry Labonte

Driver – No. 44

Kellogg's / Pizza Hut Chevrolet

What is it like going from a full schedule to just 10 races this year?

Well, not being involved in all of the races sure is different. I travel with my son, Justin, to almost all of his NASCAR Busch Series races, so I'm still at the track every week. But, the biggest difference this year is that I get to go home on Saturday afternoon. I get to sleep in my own bed most Saturday nights. Now, instead of waking up Sunday morning in a motorcoach parked in the infield, I'm waking up in my own bed.

What is it like watching your son race?

It's okay. I've found that the best place for me to watch his races is from the pit box. That is definitely the best view because I can see everything that is going on in the race. You just don't know everything that is going on if you aren't in the pits.

Do you ever give Justin advice?

Sure I do, but only when it's needed. Justin's been around this sport a long time and he's been coming to the track since he was little, so he knows what he's doing out there. Having a father and an uncle that are drivers helped him. For the most part, he knows the ins and outs of the sport.

Really, there is only so much I can say to him that he doesn't already know. But, I'm helping him out where I can.

How did you decide which 10 races you were going to run this year?

I started off by picking some of my favorite tracks. Then, I looked at the schedule and didn't want to pick races that were too close together because of the team. We went into this thing saying we were going to have a skeleton crew with only two or three cars, so we didn't want to run races that were close to one another. After I picked some of my favorite tracks, it came down to what was going to be best for the team.

Some places I miss, and some places I don't miss at all. Richmond is the track that I will miss the most this year, that's for sure. I'm thinking that maybe we'll run that one next year. Darlington is another race that I think we'll run next year, too.

But Talladega, I didn't miss that one at all. We only picked the races that we liked.

How does it feel watching your son and brother [Bobby] racing every weekend when you aren't?

To be honest, I don't really miss it. For the most part, I'm at all of Justin's races and then, I watch Bobby on TV every Sunday. So I'm still really involved.

After 2006, I'm not really sure what I'll be doing. I haven't thought much about it. ▲

". . . the biggest difference this year is that . . . I get to sleep in my own bed most Saturday nights."

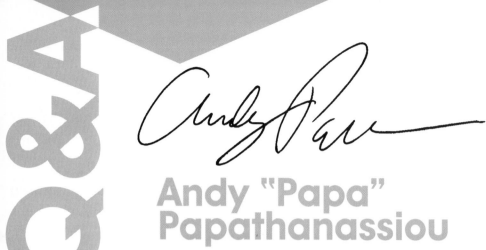

Andy "Papa" Papathanassiou

Pit Stop Coordinator / Director of Personnel
Hendrick Motorsports

What do you look for in a potential pit crew member?

We look for people who are both talented in the shop and in the pits. If a guy is a great fabricator, but hurts us in the pits, he hurts the team. Conversely, if a guy is a great athlete, but can't maneuver his way around the toolbox, he also hurts us.

Racing will find your weaknesses and exploit them very efficiently. We are not guaranteed four quarters of play, like in other sports. If we make one mistake – it could be on lap one or the first pit stop – our day is over.

Is there a single characteristic you look for?

Attitude. You want a guy who is focused on the goal and doesn't stop until he's either dead or gets there.

People look at the 12-second pit stop, but forget the context of each stop. Don't forget that each pit stop comes during a five-hour race, within the confines of an 18-hour day, at the end of a 60-hour week. You have to have guys who are consistently willing to get over those hurdles, get to Sunday and say, "Alright, it's time to go!"

Are there guys in other sports who would make great pit crewmen?

I like second basemen and shortstops because of their good hand-eye coordination and quickness. Despite being great athletes, a lot of football players are probably too big for what we are doing. We work in some pretty tight spaces. We've got two, sometimes three people in a very confined space trying to get at the same wheel.

What is the premier position in the pit?

For us, our pit stops live and die with the tire changers. They are the only guys moving throughout the entire pit stop. They're getting where they need to be, pulling lug nuts, moving a tire and getting out of the way.

Other guys can sort of get into position, take a breath, and then go to their next thing. There are little bits of time you can grab if you are a jackman, a tire carrier, or a gasman. The tire changer is "on" from beginning to end.

Rear changer is more demanding than front because the rear guy chases the car down. The car comes to the front guy.

Is there a moment during the stop when you can tell if it will be good or bad?

Certainly. How the car comes in sets the whole thing up. But today, I can tell more by listening. I can listen to the way the gun gets into the hub and hits the lug nuts, and I can tell if they are coming off the right way or not.

We take about a third of a second per lug and if you start adding a tenth of a second for lugs on and off, you can add a second per side just because you are a tenth of a second off on each lug nut.

What pit challenges do Talladega and Darlington present?

At Talladega, the car makes things difficult. Because of the way the wheel well is structured on a superspeedway car, there is sometimes just a quarter of an inch on each side of a tire. That's not a big deal if you have time to ease tires in and out, but to do that within the bounds of a competitive pit stop is very, very difficult.

Everything is designed to reduce drag at Talladega, so you've got small brakes and small rotors so if drivers don't remember to properly heat up and pump up their brakes, the cars don't stop exactly where we want them to.

At Darlington, pit road is small and congested compared to some of the newer tracks that have been built. If everybody is coming in and the cars around you are pitting at the same time as you, it is pretty crowded. If you are coming in on a green flag, you've got plenty of room and there is no problem. ▲

"If we make one mistake - it could be on lap one or the first pit stop - **our day is over.**"

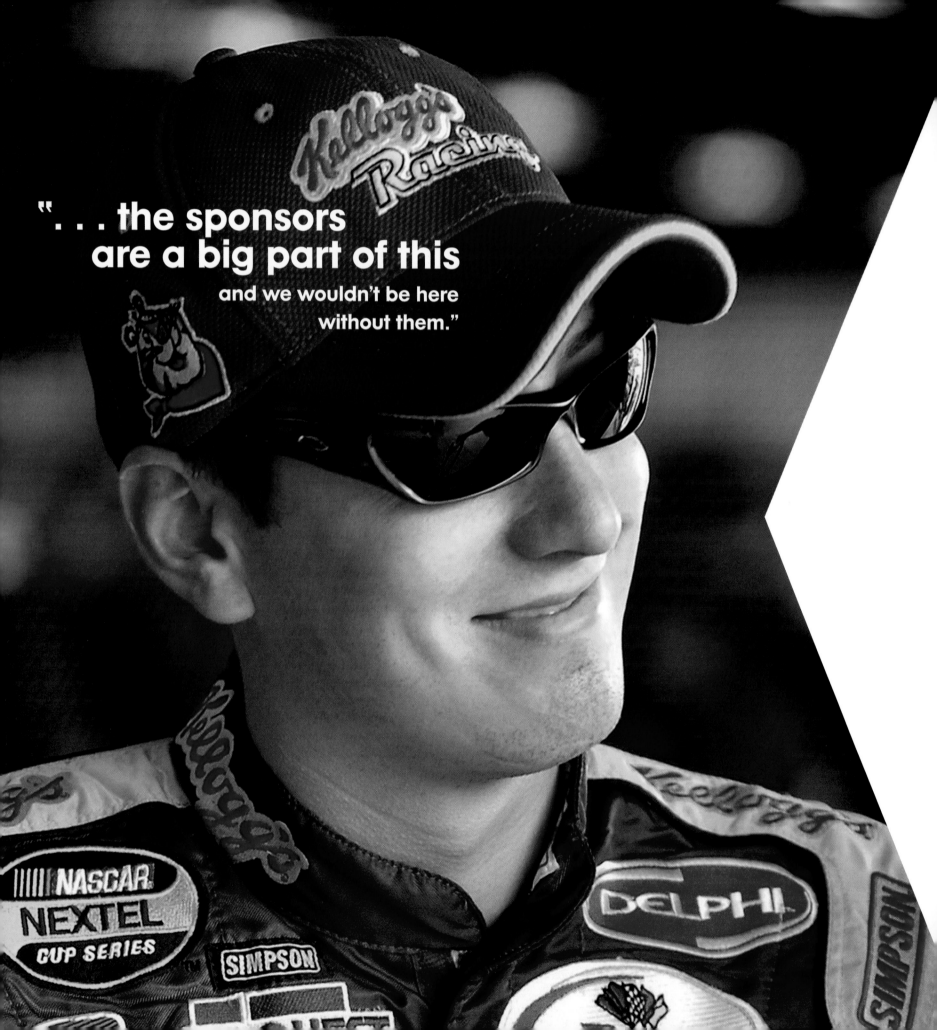

"... the sponsors
are a big part of this
and we wouldn't be here
without them."

Kyle Busch

Driver – No. 5
Kellogg's Chevrolet

How aware are you of your sponsors' role in what you do?

There was a story on *NASCAR Nation* a couple weeks ago. They featured a guy that only uses NASCAR-affiliated products – shoes, pants, shirts, whatever, it all had to be produced by a NASCAR sponsor. He'd only eat Kellogg's cereal or Cheerios and use Sunoco gasoline. It's pretty funny to see somebody that committed.

We definitely realize the sponsors are a big part of this and we wouldn't be here without them.

Was it cool for CarQuest to have a birthday party for you at Talladega?

Definitely. It was neat to go up there and for them to have a cake for me, a cake I'm sure everyone enjoyed. Of course, having everybody sing to me was pretty cool.

Did you eat the cake?

No, I didn't get a piece of the cake because we still had to go on and do one more appearance at the souvenir trailer before the drivers meeting. I went out there and signed some autographs for a bunch of fans and didn't get any cake.

Would you eat cake right before a race?

No, that wouldn't be the best idea. Although, before the race, I have been known to eat pretty much anything – whatever the guys are cooking on the truck – pork chops, tacos, whatever.

So, you've got an iron gut?

There are some guys out there, like me, who will eat just about anything. Other guys, though, are really into nutrition, hydration and carbo-loading. I actually pre-hydrate, drinking a lot of stuff the night before races so I don't have to drink a bunch on race day. I don't want to have to go to the restroom.

Do you feel the benefit of coming into the sport with Hendrick Motorsports?

Tremendously. It's been a whole whirlwind experience for me to come out here with Hendrick Motosports in the NASCAR NEXTEL Cup Series, to be associated with an organization that is out there willing to win and willing to do the best possible job that they can for you. It is a dream come true. I've never wanted anything else.

Did you come in with some built-in fans because of the Hendrick team?

Maybe. There are long-time Hendrick Motorpsorts fans. Really, I may have come in with *fewer* fans because of my association with Kurt [brother, 2004 NEXTEL Cup Champion] and not going with him and the Roush organization.

In the course of a race, are you aware that your brother is out there with you?

Of course, when he's behind me or in front of me, I always know that's my brother. I always want to race as clean as I can so that there isn't the chance of wrecking both of us.

I still want to beat him. We have a strong sibling rivalry and have for years, but we get along much better now than we did in the past. We've matured.

There's one concert you can go to, who would you see?

My two favorites are Soundgarden and Metallica.

If you had a CD player in the car, what would you listen to?

For qualifying, just to get me pumped up, rockin' and ready to go, I would crank Metallica's *Black Album* or something from Nirvana.

But for the race, I need something that could last me a while that wouldn't get me too riled up. Maybe some Phil Collins, something steady from the early '90s. Or maybe Avril Lavigne. ▲

". . . on Sunday, the guys will eat another **six dozen eggs** and **12 pounds of bacon.**"

How many different jobs do you have?

I drive my brother-in-law Brian Whitesell's [team manager, Hendrick Motorsports] motorcoach and cook for two teams at the track. During races, I'm in the pits. I hand the front tires over the wall and get the gas cans filled at the pump station. But until the race starts on Sunday, I'm at the hauler providing the meals for the guys.

What do you cook for two pit crew teams?

For breakfast on Friday and Saturday, I'll cook six dozen eggs and eight pounds of bacon. Then, on Sunday, the guys will eat another six dozen eggs and 12 pounds of bacon. I also make a hash brown casserole that has ham and sausage in it on race day. For lunch and dinner, I'll make spaghetti and tacos among other things.

Is there any particular food you don't serve before races?

Not really, but I do try and stay away from anything that is too spicy. I try to keep certain things on hand at all times, stuff that the guys all like. They really like cold cuts, so I have sliced turkey, chicken and ham and that they can make sandwiches whenever they are hungry.

Do you have a specialty?

I like making tacos the best. Tacos usually get served every weekend, either right after practice or an hour-and-a-half before the race. I try to give the guys enough time before the race so that they can eat and then we can all get changed into our race gear.

How do you make sure the guys are eating correctly?

Right now, I am working with a nutritionist to make sure these guys are getting everything they need. Our goal is to make sure they get balanced and nutritious meals every weekend.

Along with the cold cuts, I try to keep vegetables and yogurt on hand so that our guys can have something healthy to snack on instead of chips or candy.

In addition to the nutritionist, I also get input from the trainers as well as the pit coaches to coordinate what our guys are eating.

When do you find the time to shop for the food?

I usually stop at a store on the way into the track Saturday morning. But, finding stores open that early in the morning can be tough. If nothing's open, I have to go out during the day. That means fighting traffic and dealing with the crowds at the grocery store. It is not easy to duck out. You really have to time it right.

What is your operating budget?

My budget is $100 per team, per day – about $600 a weekend. Keep in mind, we get a lot of stuff from the sponsors for free, certainly cereal and drinks. I run over sometimes, but most of the time, I try to stay within budget.

RT Young

Richard Young

Cook – Nos. 5 and 25
Pit crew member - No. 5 Kellogg's Chevrolet
Motorcoach Driver for Brian Whitesell

If there is one thing the average NASCAR fan doesn't know about your job, what is it?

Most people probably don't even know a guy like me exists, but if they do, they probably don't understand how tough it can be to manage all the logistical details.

I try to pack as much on the truck before it leaves the shop as I can, but we're limited by space and by the amount of refrigeration we have. We just have small refrigerators.

I try to put as much dry and canned goods as I can onto the truck. But, I have to shop during the weekend to get fresh produce. I like to give the guys a choice of vegetables and fruits – something besides cookies and candy and that kind of stuff. ▲

"... this is it.
It doesn't get any better than this." – Christen

[Judy, left; Christen, right]

Judy Shriver

Director of Travel
Hendrick Motorsports

Christen Tinsley

Credentials Coordinator
Hendrick Motorsports

How do you prepare for the races?

Judy: My race week starts a month out, when I send the teams a preliminary rooming list. On Tuesdays before the race, I always like to send the hotels and rental car companies any changes before sending the final list out to the teams and departments by the end of the day. Obviously, there are situations where it becomes Wednesday or Thursday morning before it goes out.

Do you make changes to rooming lists?

Judy: No, we don't play musical beds. There might be a few changes but once the rooming template is set in December, we pretty much stick to that. With 130 team members, I've got too many people to deal with to have any drama.

How do you coordinate the air travel of 130 people?

Christen: I get the plane lists from the team secretaries every Monday morning. We have a pool of what we call "Flex seats" for anybody extra outside the team – i.e. people from marketing, IT or the engine department. All of our seats are allocated to a team. Once they send their lists, if there are any extras, then we compile the flex seats.

From there, it is a matter of making any last-minute changes.

Our final list is done on Tuesday, because our Busch guys fly out on Wednesday. Then, our early Cup guys go out on Thursday and our Busch late crew goes out Saturday morning and then our Cup late guys go on Sunday morning.

How many flights go back and forth during Talladega?

Christen: We have three Saab 2000s, and each holds 36 passengers. At least one will stay with the team and one will come back. Also, one will stay with the Busch team when they are traveling. That way, if there is any trouble, you already have a plane where the teams are.

Our planes will fly back and forth all day on Saturdays and Sundays but our critical flights are Saturday and Sunday mornings for the pit crews.

How do you handle travel to Darlington?

Christen: We love Darlington! We don't have to fly! The only flights to Darlington are our executive flights. And some drivers will fly their own planes down there. They may take a couple of guys here and there, but generally, the drivers handle all of their own stuff.

Do you consider yourselves members of the race team?

Judy: Definitely. On Sundays, I watch or at least listen so that I know what's going on.

Christen: Absolutely. I went to school for motorsports management, so this is it. It doesn't get any better than this. ▲

Brian Vickers

Driver – No. 25
GMAC Chevrolet

No. 24 and No. 48 had just been put together and that formula was working well. But the communication between all four teams was not quite what it needed to be. Coming into 2005, they put the No. 25 and No. 5 together across the street from the No. 24 and No. 48 and that has bridged the gap a lot.

I am also fortunate that Jimmie, Jeff and I get along great as friends. It's incredible to lean on their experience. Jeff is one of the best ever and Jimmie is phenomenal. We all have very similar personalities and that's helped me get closer to those guys. They've shown me how to handle myself outside the race track – how to manage my time so that I can stay sane at the end of the year.

As a young driver, how do you attract fans?

There are definitely people who are pre-disposed to being a fan of mine – people who support anyone associated with Hendrick. They either support the organization as a whole or they cheer for me because they like other drivers like Jimmie and Jeff.

But more than anything, you have to be successful on the race track. That's what really attracts fans. I think the biggest thing that builds fans is winning races. People like to be associated with winners.

What kind of fans do you attract?

It's different at every race track. When we go out to the trailer to sign autographs, you get a different group from track to track. The fan base you are going to have at Talladega is different than in California or North Carolina. Hey, it's pretty neat just to have fans.

It's got to be easier for you to get dates, right?

Being a professional athlete always helps. But confidence goes a long way.

Most of the time, I try not to tell women what I do – to see if it matters. I don't like to lie, but when they ask me what I do I'll say, "I sell GMAC insurance," or "I'm with GMAC."

I carry that as long as I can, until word gets out. That's why I enjoy going to New York City, or Miami. Everyone is so busy and everything is going so fast that it's easy to blend in places like that.

Most of the time, if you tell them you are a driver, they think you drive a taxicab.

Is entering the Cup Series with Hendrick Motorsports like being drafted by the defending champs?

Literally. I was fortunate enough to be drafted by a championship team. They've got great cars and great equipment but it is the people that make the difference. Hendrick Motorsports is a phenomenal organization, and it starts at the top. I couldn't ask to be in a better place.

How do you work with the other Hendrick teams and drivers?

I think the teams share more and more each year. When I first came on board, the No. 25 and No. 5 were in different shops and the

It can't be a bad thing to have women screaming your name.

No, it definitely doesn't bother me and I won't tell them to quiet down. ▲

"... you have
to be successful
on the race track.
That's what really
attracts fans."

"[The first pit stop] sets the tone for how the day is going to go."

What's it like before the first pit stop?

It is very serious. Everyone is waiting to see how the race is going. Everyone has to feel it out and once you start making laps, you see if you are going to go forward or go backwards. You have to wait to see how the race stretches out a little bit before you really get into the zone.

Is there more intensity preparing for that first one?

Yes, because you haven't done any yet that day. You haven't had any practice for two days. Everyone anticipates that first one. It sets the tone for how the day is going to go.

Do you go through the pit stop in your mind?

Oh yeah, definitely. As I get ready for that first one, I start to visualize how it should go. You have to go over what to do when you jump off the wall, stuff like that. I just take myself through what a perfect pit stop looks like.

What are the keys to a great stop?

Timing and coordination are huge. As a team, we have to be fluid and each person has to focus on being in sync with the rest of the guys.

It has everything to do with practice and chemistry. Basically, everyone knows right away if there is chemistry on a team. You can grow into it – don't get me wrong – but, a lot of the chemistry has to do with coordination, practice and getting used to somebody.

If there is tension with somebody on the team, that can throw things off as well.

What's the worst thing that can happen to you during a pit stop?

Getting hit, for sure. I got hit in Charlotte in 2003, but it wasn't that bad. My guy didn't hit me; it was another driver. It knocked me down, I twisted my ankle a little bit, but I was able to keep going. But, the next day, I was hurtin'.

In terms of routine pit stops, the worst thing I can do is lose the wheel. If I lose my grip on the wheel and it gets away from me, that's bad.

Sometimes, when I pull one out, it can get away from me. If it is a used tire and I see it, I'll go get it. I make every attempt I can to get it. As long as it stays within the inside half of the box before the car leaves, there is no penalty beyond the time we lose. It doesn't matter if it rolls across into the grass, I can go get it and bring it back.

Depending on the situation, I won't go get a runaway tire. If we are in the middle of pit road and there are cars coming, I ain't going to get it.

The penalty is sometimes one lap or it is a stop-and-go, depending on whether we are running under green or caution. It just depends, sometimes it might be a 15-second hold, but it is a big penalty.

What is the best time you've ever ripped off?

In a race, the best time we've ever had is a mid-to-low 12-second stop. That is what we want to reach.

Kevin Sigafoos

Front Tire Carrier / Mechanic – No. 25
GMAC Chevrolet

But, basically, our goal is 14 and under. That's realistic. We can do 14-flats every time.

What about practice and weight room work?

We practice two or three times per week for half an hour each time. Most of our practice is just repetition to establish chemistry on the team. Sometimes, we find things that we need to alter, things that might take off a tenth or two, but mostly it is all about repetition.

We spend an hour a day in the weight room, four times a week. For the most part, we work on general fitness. There are some things that we work on as individuals – the tire changers work on hand-eye quickness and hand speed – but as a team we work mostly on staying fit.

For me, it is mostly about arm and shoulder strength, but we also do plenty of agility and speed drills. ▲

"When it comes time to put my helmet on, it's not a job; **it's my passion.**"

Scott Riggs

Driver – No. 10
Valvoline Chevrolet

What is your mindset at Talladega?

Talladega is all about having good horsepower, a good body and the least amount of drag.

The track is wider and you have to go fast to be competitive. You don't really worry about handling because it is so wide. The car can go anywhere you want to if you put enough steering wheel to it.

You can be as aggressive as your car is good. If your car is strong, you can lean on people with air and have enough momentum when passing somebody to not only get past them, but be able to get back down in line.

You've got to take care of your car, too. You don't put yourself in a position to get torn up.

What is your thinking at Darlington?

If the superspeedways are about airflow and the draft, Darlington is all about tires. You need to take care of your tires. They are your best friends. As soon as we roll off pit road, we begin worrying about our tires at Darlington.

The surface is really like sandpaper. It just grinds the tires down. Goodyear can make tires that are harder, but harder tires have less grip and you have to have grip to go fast. I think the hardest tires we run are at Darlington and we still chew 'em up.

What makes Darlington unique?

One, you run right against the wall. When that track was designed, everyone thought cars would run on the flat part, that the banking was just there to catch you if the car got away from you. It didn't take very long, though, to find that you could carry much more speed on the corner if you stayed on the banking. So, everyone's always racing on the banking.

Another unique thing about Darlington is that there are four distinct corners to contend with. At most round tracks, you get into the corner, get off the gas, roll through the center, and back on the gas. At Darlington, you get off the gas getting in, back on the gas in the middle and back off the gas to turn again. You actually make four distinct corners just like you do at Indy.

What do you wish fans knew about your job?

A lot of the fans think that the drivers just show up, get in the car, and drive. I would love to be able to do that. It would be great. However, a good driver interacts with the whole team. He talks with all the guys on the team, makes each individual feel like part of a single unit. There can be no division or class structure – no haves and have-nots. Drivers are just another spoke, another cog in a great machine. I think my guys understand that I'm one of them. Not only have I done a lot of the jobs on the cars while I was coming up, but I still like to do them. I still understand and appreciate what they are doing.

You are competing at your sport's highest level. Is it awesome?

I'm definitely living my dream. I don't consider what I do a job. When it comes time to put the helmet on, it's not a job; it's my passion.

I feel very fortunate to even be in this position. The sport wants new, younger drivers. I think I am one of a dying breed. I came up through the ranks, putting the time and effort in, working with people, living life, buying houses, having a family and wrecking cars and bikes all over the country. Now, there are guys in their teens racing Cup.

Was there a moment when you knew you had "made it"?

I don't feel that way yet. I still drive and think – every single week – that if I don't perform and I don't run well and I don't work hard with my team, that I won't be here tomorrow. I feel that I need to continue to work at this opportunity.

Is it neat to see people with your gear on?

The first few times I was recognized in public or saw someone wearing a giant picture of me on a shirt, I was a bit shocked. But now, when I see my name or my signature, I don't think of it as me. It is a representation of the team that I happen to drive for. I don't look at that and say, "I'm the man!" I look at it and say, "That's a team – 40 people doing their best every day to make that name or that signature be better and shine brighter." My name, image and signature don't belong to just me anymore.

Is it hard for you to drive within the speed limit on the highway?

Cruise control. Cruise control keeps me from going too fast.

As a driver, you automatically, instinctively, want to push whatever you're driving as hard as it can go, until the tires can't take anymore. But, you can't do that on the road. There are a lot of people out there who don't know that their lives are in danger on the highway. I am a lot more worried about getting in an accident going from the race track to the airport than I am driving on the race track. ▲

Doug Randolph

Crew Chief – No. 10
Valvoline Chevrolet

You have to manage an entire team. What's your style?

Everybody has a different personality so I try to step back and look at each person's strengths and weaknesses. Every person has to be handled differently. Some guys enjoy it when you cuss and get mad at them; it brings out their competitive nature. Some guys love it when you pat them on the back. Others just want you to say, "Good job, man." My job is to figure out what buttons to push on each individual and then push those buttons.

Are there some tracks you prefer?

I have some favorites. I enjoy the short tracks. I grew up near Bristol, so I enjoy that one. I've always loved Darlington and have been lucky enough to work on cars that have run really well there.

Daytona and Talladega are hard on crew chiefs and crews. You have no control over what goes on, other than pit stops. We sit there watching, nervously biting our nails, and feel like we aren't doing anything. You are at the mercy of everyone else for The Big One.

What do you pay attention to at Talladega?

Talladega is all about the piece that you bring to the race track. That race is won or lost here at the shop, at the engine shop, the body shop and in the fab shop. Success at Talladega is homework: wind tunnel, engine development and testing. When we unload and make our first lap, that is pretty much all we've got. We put all our bullets in the chamber, and that's it. With NASCAR dictating the shocks and springs, we have a limited ability to work down there. So, like I say, it is all about the piece you unload.

How much do you communicate with your driver at Darlington?

We talk a lot at Darlington. Scott will get tired of me saying, "Tire management," during that race. There is a whole lot of that. Every third lap, I say, "Good lap. Tire management."

The tires fall off quickly at Darlington. If you can catch a guy and pass him in one lap, you don't hurt your tires. But, if you catch a guy and get frustrated trying to pass him and really put the car in a bind and spin the wheels, it might not affect you during the three laps you were trying to pass, but it'll hurt you the next thirty, when the right rear is gone. It is a constant reminder that, "We are racing the race track." People get tired of hearing it, but it's the truth. At Darlington, you dictate your destiny by how you take care of your tires. When the tires are new, that is the driver's opportunity to pass, and they know that. They also know that if they pass three guys and use their tires up doing it, five more are going to pass them before the run is over.

If you could change one thing about NASCAR to make the sport better, what would it be?

I would change the schedule. I know that NASCAR doesn't see it this way, but the current grind really beats up the guys who live this life.

We could run year 'round with the same number of total races but run three races a month with one weekend off each month. I think everybody would be much better off. It's not like there's an off-season anymore. We never stop. It is a constant evolution.

How does the schedule affect your family?

It is a huge sacrifice. My wife and I have been together for 12 years, so she's become accustomed to the schedule, but that doesn't mean we like it. It is real tough on the kids. My son played football one year and I got to go to all of the practices, but never a game because they were on the weekends. My daughter cheerleads and plays soccer and I got lucky this year because I got to go to her first game.

It is a struggle and it is hard on Diana, my wife, because four days out of the week, she's got to be the father and the mother. She's got to do the discipline. She's raising kids four days a week without any help.

We really have to manufacture family time. It is nice during the summer, when it stays light out until 9:00 because when I get home, we can go out on the boat and spend some time together. ▲

"Some guys enjoy it when you cuss and get mad at them . . .
Some guys love it when you pat them on the back."

Tara Gudger

Tara Gudger

Team Publicist

MB2 / MBV Motorsports

How much does your success depend on the driver's performance?

A lot. My success is very much dictated by the performance of the driver. Performance drives everything in sports, even the media. Still, I have to develop unique and different opportunities to promote our drivers. For example, on Halloween, we had a news anchor dress up in a Valvoline fire suit as a Halloween costume. You always have to come up with things like that, but for the most part, everything depends on the performance of our team.

What do you do during the race?

During the race, I'm on pit road and I run pit notes to and from TV and radio. If we are running 14th, they may not talk about us because we are not in the top five. But, if Scott comes over the radio and says something interesting about what the car is doing I can go to TV and say, "Scott says that the car is really, really tight because of X, Y or Z." Then, if they have time to fill during the race, they can look down and talk about Scott because they have information on him. So, it is just a way to get us on TV and radio.

When will you know you've been successful?

I don't know that I will ever feel that I've done everything. Obviously, it would be good to have your driver on with Jay Leno and David Letterman every night, but no drivers are like that. Every PR person out there can't expect their driver to be on the cover of *USA Today*, but they can use local TV and local radio to maximize exposure.

I don't think success is necessarily dependent on whether you are on the cover of *Rolling Stone*.

Do you market drivers or sponsors?

My job is to market our sponsors. That is the bottom line. It isn't about marketing Scott Riggs or Joe Nemechek, but those things work hand-in-hand. For example, no PR person would ever try to have an article written about Carl Edwards doing a back flip in street clothes, they are going to make sure he's got a uniform with logos on it on when he's doing the flip.

With Valvoline, a big part of my job is to make sure they are involved in anything that Scott does. And even when Scott is with fans, or signing autographs, that is still giving Valvoline exposure.

Is the constant travel hard?

It is, but it is not as hard as people think. I tell everyone, if I lived in Charlotte all the time, then I would go out with all of the same people to all of the same places. Now, I hang out with the same people, but in different places and different cities. It is just packing and unpacking my suitcase that it is a huge pain. I just got a house last year and if I had known then what I know now, I would be sure to have the master bedroom on the first floor, because I have to carry my suitcase up and down the stairs each week.

If you could tell NASCAR fans one thing they should know, but don't, about your job, what is it?

Everyone on the team is just like all the fans. You get in here and the drivers are all such nice people, so down-to-earth. They are all just guys and girls, living their dream. They are no different than anybody on the other side of the fence; they just worked hard and got the breaks. ▲

"My job is
to market
our sponsors.

That is the
bottom line."

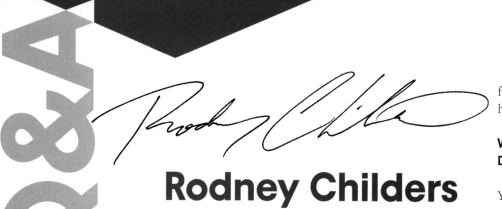

Rodney Childers

Car Chief – No. 10
Valvoline Chevrolet

What does a car chief do?

Basically, the car chief controls everything these days. The car chief is now what the crew chief was 15 or 20 years ago. Today's crew chiefs handle a lot of political and personnel matters. I make sure that what the crew chief wants done gets done correctly, and hope it all comes together at the race track.

What is your typical week like?

Monday mornings, we come in and unload the cars from the previous race and debrief. Then, they tear the cars apart and clean them up. During that time, I make notes on the computer about everything that happened over the weekend.

Then on Tuesday, we'll set up our primary car and our backup car and do a safety check on them. Then, hopefully, we load everything Tuesday afternoon and are off Wednesday until we leave on Thursday afternoon.

Weekends are pretty much a blur. You go in early Friday morning and work like crazy all day – practicing, qualifying and making adjustments.

Basically, it's the same thing all over again on Saturday, except during impound races when we can't touch the car after qualifying.

Sunday is kind of a weird deal. There is a lot of pressure on me to make sure something doesn't fall off during the race, or break. What worries me more than anything is something falling off and it being my

fault. If something falls off, I'm going to get chewed and then I'm going to have to chew somebody else.

What specific preparations do you make for Talladega and Darlington?

Talladega is all aero. You plan for speedway cars a year in advance. You are trying to get all you can get out of everything under the car, everything over the car, every little thing.

Darlington is a race track where handling is key, but it is almost a survival deal. The race track is worn out and whoever has the best car and tires at the end of the race is normally going to win.

Where can the driver make a bigger difference?

Definitely at Darlington. Darlington is all about who can get around there the best. If your car is good, that can be a good race. People always say, "If you got a rookie, take him to Darlington, he'll run good." But, the reason he'll run good is because he's crazy and willing to run the whole thing against the wall.

If you could, would you trade positions with Scott?

Scott and I have been friends forever, we used to race against each other. He tried and tried to help me out. When he was getting out of the No. 2 truck, he tried to get me in there, but they wouldn't hardly talk to me. Seems like I never got the good break other people did.

I am over being a driver, really. I just got so aggravated with it. I was really hot about it, frustrated. I guess I just wanted somebody to give me a shot. Now, I thrive on being a crew chief one day. I've got plenty of time and I'm still learning.

If you could change one thing about NASCAR, what would it be?

I would get rid of some templates. The body restrictions are out of control. It seems like they come up with new specs every week. Sure, the goal is to keep everybody equal, and maybe that is better for the fans, but I want it to be better for the guys at the shop who have built the best car. NASCAR has taken a lot of the creativity out of it.

They have 27 or 28 templates that have to fit on a race car and it takes us three hours for us to get through Tech on Friday. It's too much.

How do you balance pushing the envelope and cheating?

I'm sure that if I ever become a Cup Series crew chief, I will have plenty of fines on my side. I always try to get all I can get. Some of my late models were pretty bad. I used to win almost every late model race I went to. I was racing against guys that had 200 lbs. of lead in their cars and I had 800 lbs. in mine. But, you gotta work hard to do all that. ▲

"**The car chief** is now what the crew chief was 15 or 20 years ago."

Mike "Tuck" Tucker

Body Man
MB2 / MBV Motorsports

How did you get started in NASCAR?

A friend of mine, Glen Bobo, was working with Darrell Waltrip and the No. 17 car in 1996 and I started doing paint and body work for them. Because my daddy owned a body shop and I started working with him as soon as I was old enough, this kind of work is really all I've ever known.

When you're decaling a car, how aware are you of the value of the sponsorships?

I'll tell you one thing, you better not leave the ® for the Registered Trademark off the car. You might as well leave the whole hood decal off if you are going to leave that ® off. That is as big as big gets, man. That is a big, big deal because you never know who's going to be at the race track. The sponsors do show up and they want to see everything. Joe Race Fan would never notice the kind of stuff that makes sponsors crazy.

When the drivers tear up your work, does it bother you?

It doesn't bother me one bit. I wish the drivers would tear the front bumper and right side off every week. That means they're racin'. If the left side and the rear bumper are knocked off, he's just managed to get in someone's way. I have no problem fixin' the front and the right side. That means he's grooving and gouging.

Is what you do structural, mechanical or artistic?

I'm a glorified ditch digger, man. Bottom line, the worst two jobs in racing are body man and truck driver.

We are always the last guys to get the car and our deadlines never change. If things get behind somewhere along the line in preparing the engine or suspension, we get pressed. The end of the line is no fun. Everybody else in the shop has some wiggle room, not us.

So, you aren't an artist?

No, a trained monkey could do my job. [laughing] I think the guys that hang bodies and use the English wheel, the metalwork guys, what they do is an art. That is a talent. It takes years to master something like that. I started painting cars when I was 13 years old. It isn't exactly rocket science.

Is there another job you'd rather have on the team?

Not truck driver. [laughing] And I have no desire in the world to be a driver – that looks dangerous to me. Those young drivers have no fear, man. They are stupid. They don't know the danger.

Do you work on your own car?

No. My truck has primer all over it right now. Body guys don't work on their own cars. If you cook in a restaurant all day long, you are probably going to go home and order pizza, right? When I leave here, I just want to go to the bar or go home. My hobby is drinking cold beer and working on race cars, that is what I like to do.

When you're not at the race, do you watch on TV?

I've never missed a race. To me, if you are going to do this and don't care where you finish, you need to go work for somebody else. You don't need to be on my team. If you are just here to pick up a check, man, I've got no respect for you.

I am part of the team and the day that I don't feel part of the team, I'm going to find another team. Isn't that why we do this? That's why I got into this, because I wanted to race. ▲

"... I can't see the air yet.
**I can barely see
the gauges.**"

As a road-course specialist running only a partial schedule, how do you decide which tracks to run?

Basically, I run the races that are good for the sponsors. The races we run are in geographic areas where they do a lot of business. I have no preference. I'll race anywhere.

I do like the fast tracks, but would like to race at Bristol or Martinsville because they are cool, but right now, they're not on the schedule.

We are doing Talladega because we did really good at Daytona and have a really good restrictor-plate program.

How different is it for you to run at speedways, not road courses?

It's totally different. The things I did to win in road racing don't really apply. It is like going from baseball to football, it's basically a different sport. I am starting at ground zero. Even though I have a good feel for a race car, I need a lot of help figuring out what the car needs and how much better it can be.

I've got a lot to learn, but with good teammates like Joe Nemechek and Scott Riggs and my crew chief helping me out, the learning curve can be cut down a lot.

So, you can't "see the air" yet?

Actually, I joke about that on the radio a lot with Frankie [Stoddard, crew chief], and I get him laughing pretty hard. But no, I can't see the air yet. I can barely see the gauges. So, I've got a long way to go.

Being from out West, do you feel like an outsider in NASCAR?

Not at all. I was friends with most of these guys before I ever even got in one of these cars. I've worked with a lot of them, trying to help their road-race programs. I've tested about 18 of the top cars in the last five years and worked with drivers.

When I got to do the Bud Shootout last year, the bets were not *if* I was going to crash, but *when* and how many people I would take out with me. But, I finished the race 10th. I think that is pretty respectable. I couldn't have done that without all of the friends I made over the years giving me advice the whole time.

They don't just tell you to stay out of the way?

No, no. When they are going by me, they show me that one finger of support just to let me know I am No. 1. They've been awesome.

What is the one thing about NASCAR you would change?

That's easy, I'd add five more road courses.

What do you eat on race day?

I eat everything. I am a junk-food junkie. I eat whatever is around, a cheeseburger, a chilidog, it doesn't matter to me. My stomach is ironclad. ▲

Boris Said

Driver – No. 36
Centrix Financial Chevrolet

Terry Lane

Terry Lane
Travel / Logistics Coordinator
MB2 / MBV Motorsports
Official Scorer – No. 10
Valvoline Chevrolet

What does a travel/logistics coordinator do?

My job is a lot more difficult this year because we now have three teams (No. 01, No. 10 and No. 36). To coordinate the race, testing and appearance travel for as many as 40 people, I have to plan ahead. For instance, hotels for races are booked a year in advance and rental cars 6-8 months in advance. We mostly fly on chartered flights. Other, often larger, teams like Hendrick have their own planes, but we deal with a charter service called Racing Logistics. Choosing hotels is pretty easy. Year after year, we stay at the same hotels because the teams want to be as close to the track as possible, so once you get a foothold on a good hotel, you stay there year-in and year-out.

Do you have to deal with the dynamics and chemistry of the team?

I think that's what I really enjoy about it, touching on so many areas of the whole company. I do the credentials, crew licenses and motorhome parking credentials. The general manager has a motorhome and our crew chiefs and drivers each have a motorhome.

Are there politics with where the coaches are parked?

To eliminate some of the politics, a lot of the tracks are adopting a point system to determine where teams park.

In addition to your role in the office, you attend each race as Scott Riggs' official scorer. What exactly does the official scorer do?

I have been scoring at races since 1999 when I started doing it for Johnny Benson and I love it.

NASCAR mandates that each team have a scorer. Every car has a transponder that automatically counts laps every time it crosses the start/finish line. The scorer is more or less a back-up system in case the transponder system malfunctions.

Nevertheless, if the scorer is not in his/her seat when the race starts, the car is not allowed to begin the race, it has to sit until the scorer is in place. I've only seen that happen once.

Usually, the scorers all sit together just below the spotters' location in the grandstand tower across from the start/finish line.

Scorers each have a big sheet with slots for each lap. Every time your car goes by, you hit a little button and record the time from the official race clock at the start/finish line.

The only bad thing about it is that you cannot really watch the race. You have to watch your car at all times. Bristol is fun because you can watch the whole track and see every single thing that goes on. But at Talladega, you sit there for about a minute a lap, and it seems like an eternity waiting for your car to come back around.

What if you make a mistake?

A NASCAR official will come around and tap you on the shoulder if you miss your car. That doesn't happen to me, of course. ▲

"The first time I ever got into the garage, **I loved the people** and felt right at home."

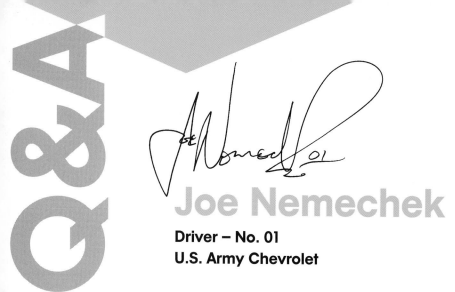

Joe Nemechek

Driver – No. 01
U.S. Army Chevrolet

For me, without those guys putting their lives on the line for us, I wouldn't be able to do what I love to do – race. It is all about freedom. Everyone takes our freedom for granted. So, it is important for me to make sure that those troops know that I support what they do, that our team supports what they do. I'm always trying to thank them.

That being said, having the Army car run good makes those guys happy. They are pulling for us.

I just want to give them something that makes doing their jobs a little easier. The tough thing for the guys on the other side of the world is that they are up at two o'clock in the morning watching our races. And there is a big group of them over there watching. To me, that is incredible. That is dedication.

What goes through your mind before a pit stop?

There are a couple different scenarios. I've been doing this a long time, so I feel pretty comfortable. No. 1 for me is to get into my pit box as quickly as possible and stop where I am supposed to stop.

The driver initiates how pit stops go. If you mess up getting in, you've ruined your whole stop. So, I want to hit my mark.

But, the main thing I'm thinking is, "Man, let this be a fast pit stop. Let me pass some of these cars I haven't passed on the race track." It is easier to pass guys in the pits with a fast stop than it is on the track.

How do you deal with mistakes made in the pits?

It gets frustrating but you have to put yourself in those guys' shoes. They didn't start the stop trying to have a bad stop. They messed up. We all make mistakes.

Everybody's great in practice. If I knew what caused bad stops, I'd be rich.

What does it mean for you to run the Army car?

People may get tired of hearing me say this, but I am extremely proud and honored to be driving the Army car. I didn't know a lot about the Army when I first started driving this car, but I do now.

Every day, my mom communicates with between 14 and 24 soldiers over the Internet. That is awesome.

What is your mom's role at the track?

During the day, my mom is out entertaining soldiers or Army VIPs. It is great to have Mom around. Heck, when she puts her Army suit on and goes out walking around, it is extra advertising for the Army, but people also look at her and say, "She's proud of what her son does." And that makes me proud.

Has racing always been a family affair?

I am very fortunate to have such a supportive family. Since I was a kid, growing up, playing soccer, baseball, football, racing motorcycles, everything we did was a family affair. We'd load the van up – or the station wagon at the time – and take off for the race track. My two brothers and I were always racing. That's what we did.

I remember one night we all went to the track as a family and all three of us got hurt. We hurt our knees. On the way home, all three of us were laying in the back of the station wagon with our knees all swelled up. It would have made a funny family portrait. ▲

"The driver
initiates how
pit stops go.
If you mess up getting in,
you've ruined your whole stop."

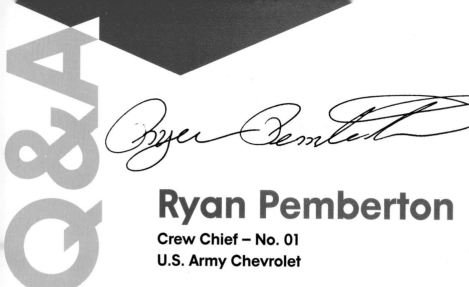

Ryan Pemberton

Crew Chief – No. 01
U.S. Army Chevrolet

Your whole family is involved in racing. How did you get your start?

My brother Robin was involved in racing his whole life and moved south from upstate New York to work for Richard Petty in the early 1980s. We just moved the whole family down.

Robin is older than me, so I looked up to him. I thought what he was doing looked pretty cool. So I used to go to the shop with him when I was just a kid and hang out with him all day. Guys would give me jobs to do like washing things, sweeping and cleaning their toolboxes. At the time, I thought it was cool. I even waxed guys' tools. I thought I was pitching in, but now I realize they were hazing me. But that's how I got my start.

What is the most important thing you do from the box at Talladega?

About every 40 seconds, I look up and watch the car go by. Then I check the TV monitor and wait for it to come by again. I just keep praying that it never stops coming by. Talladega is one of those places that will make you religious pretty quick.

It is a "car" track because you can't run fast without a fast race car. First, you need a fast race car and then, the driver has to make all the right moves.

You gotta have the whole package, it is just always easier to do it with a good car.

How different is Darlington?

It is almost a 180-degree difference. At Darlington, tires wear out in two laps. In three laps, you could be off a full second because of tire wear and rubbing the walls.

When people talk about putting a Darlington Stripe on the car, it is for real. When you run 24 inches off the wall and slide the whole time, you are going to hit it.

At Darlington, the guy who wins the race is going to be scarred up. We put different bars on the right front to keep the wall off of the suspension and off the tire. The door bars are out just a little bit, so when it rubs the wall it doesn't get the tires.

With Darlington, you worry about rubbing the wall on the right side, but at Talladega, you have to put these huge bars in the nose because they push-and-pull and push-and-pull on the straightaways. Between the two tracks, there is quite a difference in cars, philosophy and how you do things.

What goes into a good crew chief-driver relationship?

It is whatever makes the driver click. I used to be skeptical of the idea of chemistry. Years ago, before I became a crew chief, I thought "chemistry" was a load of crap. I thought, "If two guys are good, they should be better together."

It turns out there really is something to the whole chemistry thing. It has to do with confidence and trust.

How do you feel about the increasing celebrity of crew chiefs?

It is what it is. I'm not much for publicity, personally, but it's probably good for the sport. People are starting to pay closer attention to just how much goes into running race cars at the highest level. There is more to our jobs than what most people see and more to a race team than just a driver.

When somebody asks, "Who won the Super Bowl?" people say, "The New England Patriots." If the question is, "Who won the World Series?" the answer is, "The Boston Red Sox." When somebody asks, "Who won last year's Nextel Cup?" We all say, "Kurt Busch" not, "the No. 97 team" or, "Team Sharpie." Racing is the only team sport where an individual is credited for winning a title.

Taking nothing away from the drivers, it's good that recognition is breeding a greater understanding of the sport as a whole.

Do you enjoy managing people?

I personally don't think I am a good manager of people. I try to surround myself with people who don't need to be managed. I like self-motivated people.

I don't like yelling at anybody. I never liked to get yelled at myself, so I tend not to yell at anyone.

I like everybody playing like a team. We are a chain and just one weak guy can break the chain.

Sometimes though, there are people who think they have jobs that are beneath them. We went to Charlotte a while back and had moved a few people around. We had a guy who thought he should be changing tires. I told him to hold the sign that stops the car on pit road and he thought it was below him. Well, our car comes down pit road and he hangs the sign out backwards.

The blank side is showing. The driver comes right down, leading the race, but doesn't know where to stop and goes right through our pits and out the other end. The guy who thought he was too important to hold the sign screwed it up for everybody in the whole facility.

I need people who realize this is a team and that every job matters. ▲

"I like self-motivated people."

Katrina Goode

Director of Licensing & Marketing
MB2 / MBV Motorsports

As Director of Licensing and Marketing, what do you do?

I give away a lot of free stuff.

Seriously, because our team is smaller than some, we all pitch in and do a little bit of everything. I do all of our licensing, so I negotiate retail agreements. I also am the NASCAR liaison to the Charlotte office.

Jay Frye, the team's general manager, has me working with the sponsors, especially on the day-to-day maintenance of our sponsorship agreements. I also facilitate business-to-business opportunities among our sponsors, bringing them together to see if there are ways we can help them help each other.

How do you balance your drivers' and sponsors' needs?

It is difficult to separate the two – they are forever linked. Without sponsors, there are no drivers. Sponsorship dollars drive the sport. If the driver does well and becomes a fan favorite, the sponsors win. If the sponsors are happy, teams and drivers win.

We always try to put together retail promotions that will benefit the sponsors in the consumer market. That really helps our licensees see the value of being affiliated with us. Because we are not a Hendrick or DEI, we are constantly looking for ways to bring more value to our licensees.

Valvoline loves doing things with us in the retail market.

It's been a little bit of a challenge with Army because they are not a consumer brand, but still, they do a lot of giveaways at the track because their entire sponsorship is based around getting more recruits. So, they do a lot of "at-track" activation.

What is the hardest part of your job?

For me, the hardest things all stem from the size of our team.

Many of the larger teams have a line of sponsors waiting to work with them. We are constantly out there asking potential partners, "What can we do to make this work?" Whatever it takes, we'll do it.

We've got a really good group here in the front office. We don't have a lot of employees, but we all work very well together. I am always chasing down new companies to license with, increase our exposure and keep our sponsors happy.

Are you a fan of NASCAR?

I've been in this business for 10 years and when I initially interviewed for a job at NASCAR, they asked, "Who is your favorite driver?" I didn't know what to say. I'd never really watched a race. Now, I have a great appreciation for what these guys do, but I am most interested in where our guys finish. ▲

"I give away **a lot of free stuff.**"

Dave Elenz

Engineer
MB2 / MBV Motorsports

What is your job? What do you do?

For the most part, I am involved exclusively in our on-track operation. I am not at the shop doing testing like some other engineers. I am preparing to go to the race track to support the crew chief with any information he might need.

How does a young kid become you?

I was very fortunate. I decided to go to college at Clemson University to be close to the center of the NASCAR world. While in school, I went around to 35 teams looking for an internship. Only one of those teams called me back and was willing to let me work for free. If it's what you want to do, you have to put all of your work into racing. Hard work and a little luck is a pretty good combination.

If you could trade places with anybody on the team, who would it be?

Ryan Pemberton [crew chief, No. 01]. He's got it pretty good right now. He's got the big house and the boat, but has to work really hard.

I guess everyone wanted to be a driver at some point, but there is no chance. You just can't do it these days. You better be driving by age 10, and into late models by 14.

Crew chief is actually obtainable, so that's my goal.

What is your race-day job?

I calculate the fuel mileage. Hopefully, they don't need me. It's only when we are really low on fuel and we are about to run out that they need me. The thought of making a mistake on the calculations keeps me up at night.

Running out of gas at the end of a race when we're battling for a strong finish is my biggest nightmare. You get one shot to get it right and if you are wrong, you're done. It's all over.

What if the gasman spills a bunch, or the car leaves before the can is empty?

We weigh the can before and after every stop. If the catch can is filled up, we dump its contents back into the can before we weigh it. From that, we know how many gallons went into the car. We check our fuel mileage from the run before to keep a running average and that helps us predict fuel mileage for our next run.

If, for some reason, they spill a ton and the numbers look off, then you keep that in the back of your mind when it is time to get gas.

When your whole front end is cut off because of an earlier incident, what happens to fuel mileage?

Who cares? At that point, you aren't worried about fuel mileage because you pit so often. You are never going to run out of fuel while out of contention with no front end. ▲

"**Running out of gas** at the end of a race when we're battling for a strong finish is **my biggest nightmare.**"

Jeff Dowling

Race Coordinator
MB2 / MBV Motorsports

What is a race coordinator?

The race coordinator does a little bit of everything, except work on the cars. I interact with every department in the building, in some way, shape or form. I help execute sponsorship agreements and manage contractual obligations. I order uniforms and apparel for all of the teams and departments. I handle decals and I make sure that when the cars leave the shop, they are all set. If there is a change in sponsorship or a specialty paint scheme, I make sure that when the car leaves, it has everything on it that it needs. I also handle all of the credential requests for our teams.

How did you come to a career in NASCAR?

I was raised in Daytona Beach and loved racing. After a six-year stint in the military, I moved back home and started going to school while also putting in job applications all over the place, including NASCAR and the speedway.

Strangely enough, the first call that I received was to work with Bill France Sr., the founder of NASCAR. The head of security at Daytona called me at home one night and said, "I've got a little part-time job for you, but it's not much." He explained that Mr. France's health was declining and they needed help at the house. Mr. France was a big man – maybe 6'3" and well over 200 pounds. His nurses needed an extra set of eyes, ears and arms. I guess he had fallen once or twice and took a couple of people out on the way down.

I took the job and it was an amazing experience. When you grow up in Daytona, you know who Bill France is. You just know. I was with Bill every day for the last two years of his life.

When I got done with school, I held a job in NASCAR's marketing department for about nine years before leaving to work on the team level.

Do you have a favorite racing story?

It was February of 1990, my last year in the Air Force and I watched the Daytona 500 from my dorm room. I had been dating this girl for a couple of months and she asked me, "Are we really going to watch this race?" I said, "Yeah, it's the Daytona 500."

I loved Dale Earnhardt, thought he was the coolest thing ever. On the last lap of the race, he cut a tire in turn three with less than half a lap to go. Derrick Cope got under him and won the Daytona 500. I lost my mind and this girl looked at me like I was some kind of fool.

Eight years later, I was working for NASCAR and stood in victory lane with Earnhardt when he finally won that first Daytona 500. I was in marketing services at the time, so when he got out of the car, I handed him the Gatorade. On the cover of *USA Today* the next morning, Earnhardt was standing on his car with me in the background. It was awesome.

Where does race coordinator fit in the team's organizational chart?

There are workshop guys and there are front-office guys – concrete and carpet. Front-office people are the "carpet people." I am definitely one of the carpet guys.

I often act as a liaison between management and shop personnel. There are sometimes unpleasant messages that Jay [Frye, general manager] wants to deliver and I have to deal with that.

If you could switch positions with one person on the team, who would it be?

Scott Riggs. I would like to drive. Who wouldn't? Everyone wants to drive. Just some of us don't have the talent. I'd like to be Scott. He's talented, a good guy and he's got a lot going for him. We are all frustrated athletes, I guess. We wouldn't be around this sport otherwise. ▲

"Front-office people are the 'carpet people.' I am definitely one of the carpet guys."

Mike Bliss

Driver – No. 0
NetZero Best Buy Chevrolet

When you prepare for Talladega, is there anything special that you think about?

First of all, you go there pretty relaxed on qualifying day because the driver doesn't have much to do with it. It's all up to the car and crew. But race day at Talladega is a lot like Daytona because of the drafting.

Is it better to be more aggressive, or let the race come to you at Talladega?

You have to do both. In the back of your head, you think, "I don't want to be in The Big One." But if you think that way, you drive like you don't want to be in it and you'll just get in the way.

You can be aggressive and try to stay up front all day but it has a lot to do with the people around you. You can do it on your own, but when you have no friends you can get shuffled to the back only to work your butt off and get shuffled to the back again.

Does that put you at a disadvantage because you are a one-car team?

Yes. We don't have anybody that wants to help us win.

When you go to a place like Talladega, you are really a lone ranger.

I know I have no friends. The only friends I have are the ones in our crew. But you know that going in. You've got to earn respect. If you finish well one time, other teams might look at you and say, "Well, shoot. He's got a good car. We want to run behind him next time." That's where our race team is right now. Everywhere we go, we have to earn respect from the other race teams.

Is it an exciting place to race?

For the fans it is, but I don't think too many drivers would rather be there than anywhere else. I'd rather be in Martinsville or Bristol. You have a little more control over your own fate at those two.

At Talladega, you don't want to be the guy that causes The Big One. You don't want to be labeled as having caused it, that'd be worse than anything. So, you try to stay in control until the end, when it is time to race.

You've got to walk that line between proving you've got the car and not causing The Big One.

How is Darlington different?

It is a fun race track. It is one of those race tracks that has history behind it. It is like no other track and I love running there. I get tired of the tri-ovals. Darlington is about your setup, having a good team and good driving.

How do you approach taking your laps there?

You gotta think about saving your equipment. You race the track more than anything else, because that track will gobble you up in a heartbeat. You run so hard there and the walls are so close, the tires slow down and you slide around quite a bit. It is one of the hardest tracks to get your car to handle.

With the history of Darlington, what do you think about it being eliminated from NASCAR's Cup schedule?

I don't think it has long to live as a Cup track, which is unfortunate. It is one of the best. I love it. It's one of those places where NASCAR got started. You hate to see those kinds of tracks go by the wayside. It just isn't big enough and doesn't seat enough people.

How does being a single-car team affect you in the world of mega-teams?

We just don't have as many resources. For example, when Hendrick has somebody going to test at Martinsville, the other cars will feed off of what they learned. Fortunately, we have that opportunity to feed off

of what Hendrick learns because we run Hendrick engines, but we benefit to a lesser degree than their teams. On Monday morning, we don't have five crew chiefs sitting around talking about what to do. We only have one car, one crew. Bigger teams get more notes, more everything.

What do fans need to know about the challenges you guys face as a small team?

Well, this is the third year of the Haas CNC Racing team and my first year with them, so we are still growing and we hope that we are going to get better. I'm 40 and my age works against anything that will get us more attention because the attention goes to the 20-year-olds. Myself, Bootie [Barker, crew chief] and the rest of the team are all working hard to be in the mix at the end of the season. ▲

"Everywhere we go,
**we have to
earn respect**
from the other
race teams."

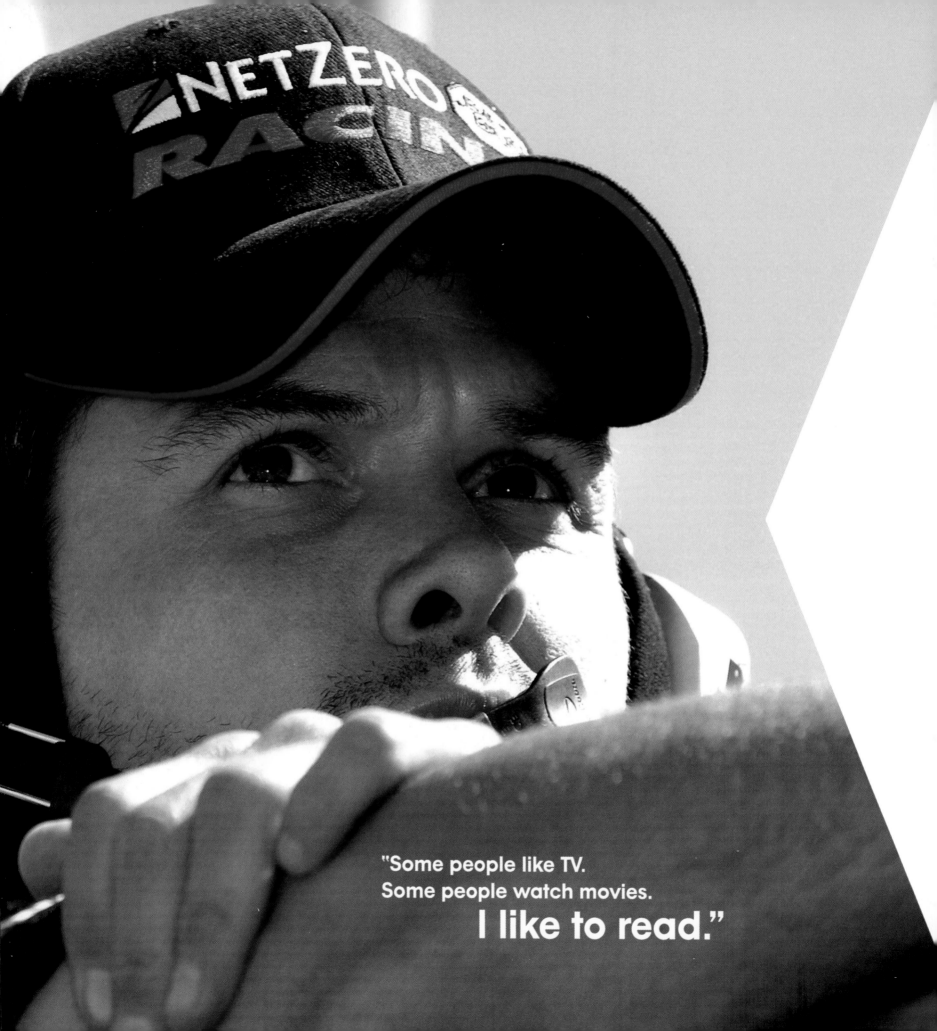

"Some people like TV.
Some people watch movies.
I like to read."

Is calling the race where you earn your money?

No, leading up to the race is where I earn my keep. You could bring in Nostradamus and he could know everything that might happen and there is still nothing you can do during the race to affect the outcome. All of the work – laying the groundwork, maximizing the car and assembling the best people – is done in the shop.

It is a whole lot easier to call a race if you have the best car, the best driver and the best crew.

How did you get your start in NASCAR?

It started when I was in college working for Ashton Lewis. Ashton Lewis Jr. is a driver and a friend of mine and then I met his father. I was studying mechanical engineering with Ashton and asked if I could work on Mr. Lewis' car for nothing and he let me. I started working on their cars at night and then going with them on weekends while I was in school.

So, when I graduated, I had some experience in the field. I came to the Charlotte area, knocked on doors and passed out resumes until I finally got in.

Is there another job in NASCAR that you'd like?

Driver, but it is not feasible that I can, so I don't think about that.

Owner? The best way to make a million dollars in racing is to start with a *billion*. So, I don't know that the allure of ownership would be there for me.

Realistically, in terms of the things that I could possibly do, I've kinda reached it. I just want to keep getting better at what I do and win more races.

How has the emergence of crew chiefs as celebrities affected you?

We make more money now. I've heard *Mo' Money, Mo' Problems* but I don't see P. Diddy giving any of his money back. I'd rather have to decide between filet mignon and rack of lamb than wonder, "Am I going to eat today?"

I don't know if crew chiefs deserve all the attention we're starting to get. Our role has expanded, but the driver is still the most important element in any team. If you don't have a good wheelman, you are never going to succeed. As tight as it is now and as good as the teams are, a team can't carry an insufficient driver.

Besides being able to pay more bills, do you like being a celebrity?

I don't mind it. You hear so many people, like movie stars say, "I just want to be left alone." If that is the case, why are they making movies? Why do they show up at premieres? Why are they so wacky? You can't have it both ways. Because fans like me, I have been able to do

Robert "Bootie" Barker

Crew Chief – No. 0
NetZero Best Buy Chevrolet

some TV shows, and that's allowed the sponsors to get to know me better. That might even help me keep a job down the road.

Could you have imagined, when you were getting into racing, that you would rise this fast?

That is what you dream about, that is what you work for. It didn't take long for me to figure out that if you ain't the lead dog, the view never changes. Pretty quickly, I started figuring out who did what and who answered to whom and started formulating a plan to get to where I wanted to be – which was crew chief. However, when you get to be crew chief, you still have bosses – just not as many as other guys.

The main reason I wanted to be a crew chief, though, is that I enjoy the challenge of making cars go fast.

How much of your success is directly attributed to your degree in mechanical engineering? How much is experience?

Most of this is actually doing it, but you have to be smart. You have to be able to take in what you see around you and adapt. You have to be able to recognize things and generate ideas. A guy off the street might not understand downforce, drag or aerodynamics, but if he is smart, experience will teach him.

How closely do you work with the sponsors?

I do whatever they want me to do. I will make appearances and such, but I don't feel too comfortable doing it because I feel the driver should be the face of the team. I do not ever want to be more of a personality or have more publicity than the driver. If the sponsor wants me to do something, as long as the driver is not offended, I will do it. ▲

"[Getting payroll done] is my top priority at the beginning of each week.

If I don't get that done on Monday, the guys are very, very unhappy."

What is your role at Haas CNC Racing?

In addition to handling all the team travel, I am the human resources manager and take care of benefits, hiring, payroll and accounting. Since this is a small team, we all have more than one job to do.

When is payday?

I try to get payroll done on Monday. That is my top priority at the beginning of each week. We pay the guys weekly. If I don't get that done on Monday, the guys are very, very unhappy.

What is the biggest travel nightmare you have to deal with?

You never know where the guys are going to leave the rental cars. Often, the best race of the weekend is the one to the airport after the race.

These guys want to get home after a long weekend at the track and sometimes the rental cars are left at baggage claim. Sometimes, if there's really bad traffic and the airport is close, like in Daytona, they'll leave 'em on the side of the road and just walk. On a really good day, all the cars get returned to the rental car company. One time, our car chief came in on a Monday morning and said, "Before you hear it from somebody else, there is something I need to tell you. We had a little incident with the rental van last night coming back to the airport." Not knowing what was coming next, I said, "Okay…" He said, "Well, we kinda ripped the door off of it and just left the door where it landed and went on to the airport."

And I said, "You did what?"

Do you handle rooming lists?

Oh yeah. And there can be some drama. It isn't really political, but sometimes guys want to change roommates. They'll say, "I don't wanna room with him because he snores," or, "He runs around in his underwear, can I bunk with somebody else?" The guys are very picky about their roommates. Usually, they will team up at the beginning of the season and I'll just keep it that way for the rest of the year. Generally, the guys will come to me only if they have a problem.

What do you enjoy most about your job?

I enjoy the people I work with and the fast pace of this industry. I don't like to be still and the time flies by here.

In fact, I don't really see this as work. Sure, I get paid for it, but it is totally different than other jobs. I actually look forward to getting up and coming to work in the morning. You feel like you have a reason to come to work because you are helping somebody else. This is a team sport.

Donna Swartz

Business Manager
Haas CNC Racing

What do you think of NASCAR's desire to add international races?

I do foresee the Cup Series heading to Mexico soon. Because we did it this year in the Busch Series, the hard part is out of the way. NASCAR was amazing with their planning and support. I never could have imagined the trip would be so smooth. The biggest challenge for us was finalizing our manifest. You don't fully understand what kind of inventory is carried on those trucks every week until you're asked to make an itemized list of its entire contents. You take it for granted when you don't have to account for it. I was on the phone with our driver as he was crossing the border, asking, "Did you have everything counted? Did you make it?"

How important is having a team plane?

I don't see how a team could go without their own plane. Even eight or nine years ago, when I worked with Rudd Performance Motorsports, we had our own plane. Whether you have one team or 20 teams, you can't function in this industry, if you don't have your own air transportation. ▲

Michelle L. Marckwardt

Michelle Marckwardt

**Communications Manager
NetZero Best Buy Racing**

How did you get your start in NASCAR?

Even as a little girl, I knew I wanted to be in racing. Because I never learned to drive a stick and wasn't much of a gearhead, I went to Michigan State and got a marketing degree. My hope was that I could land a job on the business end of racing after graduation. However, somewhere along the line, I wound up working at Kmart – not exactly the road I was trying to take.

Several years later, I was like, "Whoa, this isn't right. This isn't what I want to do." So, I sent out probably 250 resumes for jobs in all levels and forms of racing and got two responses. One of the replies came from Roush Racing and they hired me.

I grew up an Indy car fan and I had never even been to a NASCAR race until I went to college. Now nine years later, I can't imagine doing anything else.

What exactly do you do for Haas CNC Racing?

I actually work, not for Hass, but for the agency hired by NetZero Best Buy to promote the team.

My whole focus is publicity. There are other people who handle the pit tours and other sponsorship stuff.

If I worked for a driver who consistently ran in the top five, year after year, my job would be to manage publicity requests. But here, I figure out what I have to work with each week and use whatever leverage or story I have to promote the team. I handle Mike Bliss' schedule and try to get the NetZero Best Buy message out there. I end up doing a lot of writing. I write the pre- and postrace reports that go to the sponsors and media.

Is it tough to judge how intrusive to be during race weekend, when Mike is trying to prepare himself mentally for a race?

Yes, and every driver is different. Mike [Bliss] is probably the easiest driver that I have ever worked with. I always try to stay out of the way. I am probably less intrusive than I could be, but I try to respect the fact that he is there to work, the team is there to work and then, if there is time, I will set stuff up.

Honestly, most of my work is done during the week. By the time I get to the race track, everything is set up; I know exactly what I need to do. Obviously, things will come up – somebody always needs something from Mike. But I work really hard during the week, to keep from scrambling on race day.

If something is going on in your pit or garage, is it your job to get the media interested in coming over to cover your team?

During a race, after an accident, I've had a couple of drivers say to me, "Go get TV. I want to talk to TV." They obviously had something on their minds that they wanted to share...with everybody.

Honestly, a lot of times, I don't ever see TV and it wouldn't matter if I were chasing them down, they still wouldn't come and talk to us. Until we can get ourselves running consistently every week – and we are well on our way to doing that – this is the way it is going to be and what I struggle with most.

Is that one of the biggest challenges in promoting a small team?

I can talk to TV crews all day long, but if they are not showing our pit stops, then they aren't talking about us. During a race, every time we come in for a pit stop, every time we hear something on the radio, I feed it to TV. That is my job during the race – to feed information to TV and radio. I can go 500 miles feeding them stuff after every pit stop, about every change we made, and I'll go back and watch it on TV and see none of it. That is very frustrating, but it's my job. It's just tougher for small teams.

If you are one of the big boys, like a Hendrick or DEI, TV is sitting in your pit covering every breath you take. You don't need to chase them down.

From a publicity perspective, when will you know that the team has "made it"?

When I *take* more calls than I make or when I go out for qualifying and there are 43 cars there and TV wants to talk to my driver. They do it now, but not all the time. And, there are some drivers, who before they even qualify, have radio, TV and newspaper waiting to talk to them.

When newspapers that only cover regional races start thinking they've, "got to talk to Mike Bliss," that's when I'll know that we've made it. ▲

"Even as a
little girl,
I knew I wanted to be
in racing."

"If he can hold a steering wheel and **mash the gas pedal for a win,** that's the guy for me."

What is your role as team manager?

After bouncing between being shop foreman and crew chief for both our Cup and Busch teams, they made me team manager.

With that, I attend all of the morning meetings and if I have something to say, I do. If not, I just let the shop foreman handle the meeting, laying out the day's work.

How do you approach Talladega and Darlington?

At Talledega, you need a fast race car, a slick car that cuts through the air. It needs to be able to get down out of the air.

Darlington is way different. There, you run two laps and don't have any tires left. Darlington is about tire management and shock absorbers.

You can't stay off the wall at Darlington. If you are smart, you can use the wall to show you how to best get around the track. Just get up there and run with it. We actually put an extra roll bar out past the sidewall of the right-front tire. That way, you can get out there and rub that bar all day long without hurting the tire. We've come back with our side cut in two where the wall rubbed the sheet metal right down to the bar. But, we didn't have any suspension damage or anything. We ran all day long.

What is your favorite part of the job?

Besides payday? Frankly, I like working with people. I like problem solving. I enjoy answering the guys' questions about racing, personal issues, whatever.

Joe Gibbs helped me get to this point and doesn't even know it. He interviewed me for his team when he originally started it. He said that when one of his players was having trouble, he would follow the player home, and there he'd usually find the root of his problems. He would deal with his players on a personal level, remembering that each member of his team also lived a life outside the team.

All I did was interview with the guy about a job and he taught me something that I use to this day.

In management meetings, I stress that the most valuable resource we have is our people. Every team has money to buy motors, gears, bodies and chassis. We can all buy those things. We can't buy people.

Which is harder, preparing a car or preparing people?

People. The car is easy. It's just dumb metal. If you beat on it long enough, it'll do just what you want. You can't do that with people because everyone has a different personality. Cars may have personalities too, but you can guide them and they don't talk back. They either run or they don't. Building a team of people is much harder than building cars.

How do you get two guys who have had a falling out to trust each other again?

With the pit crew, normally once they go to a couple of workouts together and realize they are each giving 100 percent, they wipe the slate clean and knock the chip off their shoulders and go on about doing their jobs. Very rarely do we have situations where someone quits or is fired

Bill Ingle

Team Manager
Haas CNC Racing

over a dispute from pit road. Pit road is a battle, and we've all heard of things happening in the "heat of the battle." Normally, once we get back here on Sunday or Monday, we all forget about it.

What is your role on the weekends at the tracks?

At the race track, I go with the Busch team. I am an integral part of the Busch team helping the crew chief and engineers make decisions about what to do with the car and the people. I try to make sure we are working together and everything is flowing.

Then, on Sundays, my other new job is spotting for Mike [Bliss].

What does a spotter do?

Basically, the spotter's role is to keep the driver informed of what's going on in front of him. As a former driver and crew chief, I can stand up there and feed the crew chief and driver information about how other cars are racing. You watch the lead car – if you are not it – and see if he's running a different line. Then, you tell your driver, "Look, the leaders are running here or there and their lap times are quicker than yours. Try changing your line." There is a lot that goes into being a good spotter.

If you can tell that two guys are getting in an accident, tell the driver to be "heads up." Most of the time, the best thing to do is just say, "Crash" and let him guide himself through the crash. If you try and guide him through it, 90 percent of the time, you'll drive him right into it. The driver gets paid to drive, let him drive. Tell him what happened and then let him make that decision. If you can give him some guidance, okay, but it is better to let him make the decision.

Are you at all concerned with the influx of ever-younger drivers into NASCAR?

No. I like the young, ballsy drivers – even if they don't know anything about cars.

I would rather have a gutsy driver that *drives*. I don't care if he can't weld or even drill a hole for a pop rivet. If he can hold a steering wheel and mash the gas pedal for a win, that's the guy for me.

I like the guy who is balls-out when he straps his helmet on. ▲

"The adrenaline,
the teamwork,
that is my addiction;
that is my drug."

What is your role with the team?

I drive the hauler and during races, I'm the gasman.

On Fridays and Saturdays I help work on the car at the track. Whenever one of the mechanics turns around, I try to know what he needs, and have it ready. If we are going to do a gear change, I know what gear is going to go in the car, up or down, so I have the gear there, with the gear oil. So, when Bootie [Barker, crew chief] says we are going to change to a 5/11, *boom*, it's already there. To me, that is what a good truck driver does.

Someone said truck driver is the worst job in racing because every delay will affect you and your deadlines never change. True?

Trying to drive from here to Texas, after you got the car late on Wednesday and need to have it there Friday morning at 5:30 a.m., is tough.

I've left for Daytona and driven straight through the night without a shower, without washing my face, without eating, then pulled up, parked and gotten right to work. That's what is so cool though.

When I am on the road on the way to New Hampshire at 4:30 in the morning, I've got 83 people and all of our sponsors counting on me to get there safely and on time. I trust my guys with my life and they trust me with their livelihood and their careers. If you were an athlete during any portion of your life, you can't live without that feeling.

When driving, are you aware of how much your hauler is worth?

I think about the value all of the time. There is nothing you can do if you wad that thing. Our sponsors don't want that kind of publicity, with pictures of the hauler on the side of the road. That is where the buck absolutely stops. I can't afford to make a mistake. Our driver can wad a car in practice and we have a backup. There is no backup hauler. That's what I like, though, that the team is counting on me and trusts that I'll get everything to the track, safe and sound.

What makes you good at what you do?

My reputation is that I can get anything legal in three minutes or less. That's my job. I have to have a rapport with everyone in the garage. I can literally go onto the No. 24 truck and grab a lower A-arm if I need to. I can go onto the No. 10 truck and grab a pair of shocks if I have to. Those are the relationships that I have to have. After we crashed once, I ran over to our truck and there were five other truck drivers asking, "What do you need?"

This is a small fraternity. If you go out of your way to help others, others will help you. Once, the No.

Robby Maschhaupt
Truck Driver and Gasman – No. 0
NetZero Best Buy Chevrolet

29 borrowed 10 gallons of regular generator gas from my truck during the race. They just went and got it and then, the Monday after the race, the fuel was sitting at my house when I got home from work. You just can't get that in the real world.

What's the best part of your job?

Going over the wall is the best part, because that is the rush for me. Sometimes this sport is ugly because the truck drivers can be segregated as bottom feeders. I'm not a truck driver. I drive a truck.

Gassing the car is by far the best part of my job because it is the easiest and provides that adrenaline rush. The pressure is awesome. If you make a mistake, everyone knows it. You've got to be willing to take chances. A ship is safe in the harbor, but that's not what a ship was made for.

What is the worst thing that can happen for you on a gas-and-go?

To not get the car full before they are ready to go. You can be slow to the car, spill too much, or hit the side of the car.

If they are going to take on two tires, you have less than six seconds and it takes just about six seconds to dump 11 gallons. Your better gasmen get to the car in less than a second. So if it takes 6.5 seconds per can, that's 12.5 -13 seconds right there, dumping the can. So, if your guys are ripping off 13.5s all day, the gasman better be on his game.

What does every NASCAR fan need to know – but doesn't?

That it is not nearly as glamorous as they think it is. It is a lot of hard work and sacrifice.

I've never had kids because I give everything at the shop. My wife works for Hendrick Motorsports as a flight attendant. She flies to the same cities I'm in every weekend, but we're in different hotels and never see each other. ▲

"Darlington is all about survival."

Rodney Childers
Car Chief – No. 10
Valvoline Chevrolet

DARLINGTON AFTER DARK
Still Too Tough To Tame

nly six days after Talladega and The Big One, Darlington faced a weekend of activity punctuated by question marks. How would fans take to the first night race – and only race of the season – at the track? Does NASCAR still have room in its schedule for the venerated track? Can the notorious egg-shaped oval still compete with the new tracks out West?

It didn't take long to see that The Lady in Black still had some fight in her. A clear, crisp evening provided the perfect back-

drop for the Dodge Charger 500. Darlington gave the drivers – and the sold-out crowd of 60,000 raucous fans – all they could handle.

We watched our drivers earn their Darlington Stripes the hard way and learned just how quickly the gritty track devours tires. Following a thrilling finish, everyone – from the fans in the infield to the drivers running two laps down – seemed determined to savor their only visit to the track that is Too Tough To Tame.

Night moves: The NASCAR NEXTEL Cup Series' first-ever night race at Darlington.

EARLY ACTION
Practice Features Rain and Pain

ABOVE: This is why they call Darlington The Lady in Black.

OPPOSITE: After several drivers picked up a Darlington Stripe in qualifying, the wall needed a makeover.

After a rainy Thursday, NASCAR teams squeezed in a Friday-morning practice session and a qualifying run later that evening.

Not surprisingly, it didn't take long for The Lady in Black to claim her first victim. With only a few minutes remaining in practice, Mike Bliss lost control of the No. 0, slid into the interior wall in Turn 2 and severely damaged the front

end. After posting the 12th-best practice time, the No. 0 team was forced into an untested backup car and qualified 29th.

Once the starting order was set, NASCAR's new impound rule came into effect and all cars were shrouded and the garage closed. Though the green flag was still a day away, last-minute adjustments would have to wait until after the race had started. ▲

OPPOSITE: Robby Maschhaupt parks the NetZero hauler. TOP: And so it begins: The haulers head into the infield.

ABOVE LEFT: The No. 10 car endures an early inspection. ABOVE RIGHT: The Haas team tries to keep the No. 0 car dry.

www.millerind.com

ABOVE: The NetZero car comes in after a wreck during practice.

RIGHT: Mike Bliss, Bootie Barker and other members of the NetZero team huddle in the garage area.

OPPOSITE: "At Darlington, the type of asphalt they used to make the track seems to have a lot of glass in it and it tears the tires all to hell." – Bootie Barker

ABOVE: The cover-up.

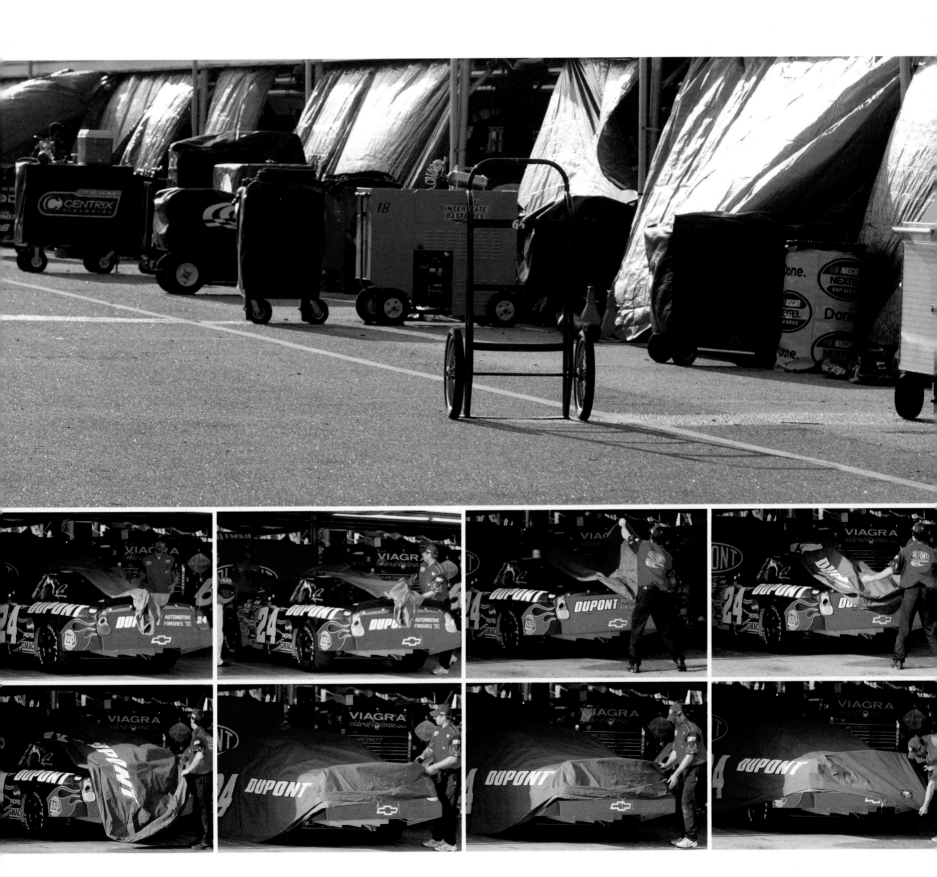

TOP: Impound. BOTTOM: The No. 24 gets tucked in for the night.

ABOVE: With Mother's Day just a few hours away, NASCAR and the drivers celebrated with their moms.

RIGHT: A full house for the drivers meeting.

OPPOSITE: Before getting into the car, Jeff Gordon pauses for prayer.

INTO THE NIGHT
Teams Challenge Track, Battle Wall

In a back-and-forth contest that wore drivers down as relentlessly as it devoured tires, the Dodge Charger 500 was exactly what fans came to see. It didn't take long for Darlington to live up to its ornery reputation. Before the field turned 10 laps, two caution flags had already come out. After that, however, the race settled into a chess match with teams saving their treads and keeping their cars off the wall.

Jimmie Johnson, Jeff Gordon, Joe Nemechek and Brian Vickers all managed to lead at least one lap during the race, with Gordon finishing a strong second. After starting at the back of the field, Mike Bliss managed to coax his back-up car to a top-20 finish.

However, not everyone could overcome Darlington's challenges. Scott Riggs battled handling problems throughout the race and was helped into the wall on lap 242. Kyle Busch was contending for a top-5 finish when he cut a tire and wrecked 100 laps short of the checkered flag. ▲

OPPOSITE: Dusk in Darlington: The grandstands are packed for the race.

ABOVE: Not a Kodak moment: Travis Kvapil pins Scott Riggs to the wall.

Organized chaos: The Army over-the-wall crew races to complete a sub-13 second pit stop.

ABOVE: As the sun sets and the track cools, the action heats up.

RIGHT: Quick hands: Jimmie Johnson gets the go-sign.

BELOW: Jeff Gordon beats Dale Jr. off pit road.

INSET: Hot wheels: Teams burn off worn rubber to gauge tire performance.

ABOVE: Gotta make the donuts.

INSET: Greg Biffle takes the checkered flag for his third win of the season.

MAMA, I'M COMING HOME
Darlington Sends Everyone Packing – With Work To Do

ABOVE: The No. 10 car limps back to the garage.

OPPOSITE: An evening of fireworks concludes with a *bang*.

As Greg Biffle celebrated his last-lap win, our teams took stock of their late-night dance with The Lady in Black.

The No. 01 team underwent a random postrace inspection while trying to get to the bottom of a late-race "tap" that nearly wrecked their Army Chevrolet.

The No. 10 team, bent but not broken, loaded the hauler and hoped the sun would, indeed, come out tomorrow.

Mike Bliss enjoyed a top-20 finish, despite being relegated to a back-up car. For the Hendrick teams, perspective reigned supreme.

Jeff Gordon found some solace in a second-place finish while Jimmie Johnson rested easy knowing that his seventh-place finish was good enough to keep him on top in the points standings. For Brian Vickers and Kyle Busch, just finishing at Darlington was good, but doing so in the top 25 was a real accomplishment.

While our teams packed the trucks for the relatively short ride home to Charlotte, preparations were well under way for Richmond, the next stop for this speed circus.

We too prepared for the next step in *our* adventure, knowing that we would enter our offices on Monday morning faced with the challenge of putting this book together. After spending the better part of a month with these teams, doing research, attending meetings and following their every move, we were excited to get started, but wished the ride had been longer. ▲

OPPOSITE: Dan Kendrach returns the Black Box to an official.

ABOVE: As a top-5 finisher, the No. 24 car gets checked after the race.

LEFT: Rick Hendrick, Ryan Pemberton and Joe Nemechek discuss the finish.

BELOW: Final exam: The No. 01 car goes through the random postrace inspection.

OPPOSITE: Ryan Pemberton and Joe Nemechek discuss a late-race bump that almost wrecked the car.

ABOVE: Brian Vickers shakes hands with his crew before heading home.

ABOVE: The Valvoline trailer leaves the infield.

All photos by Phil Cavali (philcavali.com).

Except the following:

Fluharty, Jim: 147 (sequence and top), 166

Fresina, Michael: 25 (upper left), 26 (bottom three and middle left), 74, 95, 110, 144, 145, 156 (bottom)

Huneycutt, Jeff: 45 (top and bottom left), 54-57, 100, 101

Mattila, Bambi: 63, 75 (top), 95, 148 (top), 154, 156 (top), 157 (top)

NASCAR Media: 3

Porter, Randy: 22

Robinson, Jeff: 151, 159

Sluder, Mark: 154, 169 (bottom), 141, 149, 150, 161, 162 (bottom), 165

Special thanks to David Griffin, Shea Alexander and the entire *NASCAR Scene* staff for their support and enthusiasm.